干

高 层 著

杯

葡 萄 酒 人 物 志

序言

上海日报 总编辑

吴正

约莫七年之前，受朋友的朋友之托，译过一本有关葡萄酒的非虚构类文学作品。但却由于种种原因，译稿一直没能付梓。花了大半年的时间，最后只换来电脑里的一个文档，当然有些心塞。唯一可以聊以自慰的是，这本书让我窥探到了一个葡萄酒的世界。

更确切地说是上个世纪八十年代末到二十一世纪初名贵葡萄酒的世界。那里活跃着各种有钱有闲的葡萄酒爱好者，从酿造到销售到拍卖的各类葡萄酒专业人士——传统的西方豪门名流，崛起的东方新贵。各色人等，围绕着一瓶据说是美国第三任总统、有着"美国葡萄种植业之父"之称的托马斯·杰斐逊所藏1787年法国拉菲而依次登场，演绎出一个有拍案惊奇效果的故事。

那个故事其实还没有结束。据媒体报道，书的作者，一个GQ、《美食美酒》等杂志的自由撰稿人，因此被告上了法庭。冗长的诉讼是否已经完全终结虽然不得而知，但书的版权早就被电影制作公司相中将搬上银幕。一度传说主演是布拉德·皮特，最新的消息是马修·麦康纳已经接拍，电影会在2017年上映。

在翻译的过程中，我曾闪过这样的念头：红酒圈的人物，红酒圈的故事，尤其是过去十年中经历了狂飙式发展的中国红酒业，对于记者来说，是多好的素材库啊。

首先，和酒亲近的人，多半是我们在日常生活中觉得有趣、有意思、有阅历的那些人。有一种说法，爱吃甜食的人一般脾气都不错，我想爱喝葡萄酒的人多半内心都想追求一种更美好的生活方式吧。据说一个丹麦的医学博士为此还专门做过调查，发现爱喝啤酒者智商平均值为 95.2，而爱喝葡萄酒的人智商平均值则是 113.2。因此调查的结论是：葡萄酒爱好者拥有更高的情商，也具备更好的环境适应能力。看来，成功人士喜欢葡萄酒绝非偶然，因为葡萄酒不仅让他们身体健康，聪明且有情调，还能让他们多赚钱！调查结论是否科学姑且不论，翻翻高层这本书里的人物背景，比如说牛津大学数学系毕业的 Jancis Robinson、加拿大多伦多大学物理系毕业的吕杨，他们的人生轨迹，是怎样离开了那些支撑和改变世界的高端科学领域，而滑落到这个玄妙、充满灵性的红酒世界里的呢？这样的故事，真的很好读。

其次，诚如本书中林裕森先生所言：葡萄酒的世界里到底哪些是真实的哪些是骗术？越来越发现两者间的界限很模糊，答案一直在变。正因为这种模糊和变化，在对葡萄酒的审美过程中，人的想象力得以充分发挥。对于葡萄酒品鉴的描述，进而对于葡萄酒这一产业的想象余地，也因此变得格外广阔，这也使得葡萄酒产业和其他产业相比，显得更为有趣。在那本没能出版的翻译小说里就有类似的描述：有个品酒师能够"在每一杯葡萄酒里看到女人的身影"，有一瓶酒让他觉得"你可以仰慕她们，但你并不想和她们上床，"而另一瓶酒则让他想到了"中学生的制服"。

最后，我相信中国近年来的红酒圈，将是一个蕴藏着各种故事的大宝库，有待作者们的追寻和发掘。在短短几十年间，国人对于喝红酒这件事的认知，有着不可思议的飞速发展——从只认识张裕、长城、王朝三个红酒品牌，跨过兑雪碧喝红酒的阶段，成为广大中产阶级心目中的必要修养。这一路走来，有多少杯酒人生值得被抒写，被传扬。

一年多前的某个中午，就着一杯香槟，在上海某个街角的小餐馆里，我和高层就聊起了这个话题。那个中午，也就是本书集纳的这些文章的由来。

在这些文章的采写过程中，高层自己也已经成长为一个不折不扣的红酒鉴赏者。在此，我祝愿高层，在红酒的世界里挖掘更深更好更精彩的故事，同时也成就属于她自己的独特的人生故事。

目录

后记

中国酿酒师的
等待

对于自己的职业，酿酒师李德美有一个有意思的阐述。他说，每一个酿酒师都有魔法，能把一年的阳光、土壤、雨露通通装入酒瓶里。一瓶来自中国宁夏的葡萄酒"加贝兰 2009"成就了这个拥有魔法的中国人。

Meet
the maker
of
China's top wine

这是酿酒师李德美最爱的照片之一：他半躺在长城的烽火台上，把五瓶法国的葡萄酒纳入怀中，分别是 Margaux, Cheval Blanc, Petrus, d'Yquem 和 salon 香槟。他的身后是延绵起伏的山峦，山峦上的天空似是被大漠的沙土蒙上了层纱，依稀勾勒出长城蜿蜒的曲线。面对镜头，他浅浅地笑，有些醉意。

这不禁让人想起唐朝诗人王翰的《凉州词》："葡萄美酒夜光杯，欲饮琵琶马上催。醉卧沙场君莫笑，古来征战几人回。"

葡萄酒行业中的爱国主义者总喜欢用这首诗来表达中国酿造葡萄酒的源远流长。可这纯属自欺欺人，诗里所谓的葡萄美酒是一种西域特产，和我们现在所讨论的葡萄酒风马牛不相及。

"严格算起来，中国葡萄酒业的发展历史从 1997 年开始，在这之前，半汁葡萄酒不能算是真正意义上的葡萄酒，写这一段的时候，你措辞不要过于激烈啊！"李德美说道。

这篇文章，完全没有刻意要把李老师写成爱国英雄的意思，但他对于中国两个字的在乎已到了下意识的程度。很明显，2011 年的那场加贝兰风波让他在措辞上变得更加小心谨慎。那次风波源于 Decanter 杂志在伦敦举办的葡萄酒大赛，那是全球最为瞩目的年度盛事，也让李德美一夜成名。

Winemaker Li Demei compares himself to a glass of Domaine Chevalier, saying both he and the wine are "low-key and implicit enough to be easily missed, but recognized as a top Bordeaux white due to its depth and profundity."

The 43-year-old winemaker, a native of Shandong Province, says his greatest pleasure is using his "wine language to establish a dialogue" with the wine drinker.

为了公正，大赛组委会为每一瓶参赛酒套上了个黑色的绒布袋，以避免个别势利眼的评委看到那些名庄酒标就不假思索地打上个高分。每个评委每天要品尝上百款酒，时间一长，他们脸上有了倦意，露出一丝烦躁。就在这个时候，每个人的酒杯又被倒入了一款红酒。他们努力地保持着专业，观色，摇杯，把鼻子伸到杯子里去，不放过一丝香气的表现。评委们的表情发生了明显的变化，有狐疑的，有好奇的，有不解的，很多人闻了又闻，品了又品。这酒太特别了，和他们这辈子尝过的所有产区都不同。

"雄浑的酒体，成熟的黑色水果香气中夹杂着薄荷和干树叶的芬芳"。评委们写下他们的评语。

This language, in his words, "transcends time and space," describing the climate of the vintage, whether the summer is hot and dry and the winter frozen, whether the vineyard grows on a misted mountain or beside a beautiful river, whether the soil is rich in clay and mineral content.

Li, one of the first French-trained Chinese winemakers, established his name on the world stage in 2011 when his Jia Bei Lan 2009 produced in northwestern China's Ningxia Hui Autonomous Region won a top global honor in a blind tasting, the highest award ever given to a Chinese wine. Li's blend of reds from northwestern China received the Red Bordeaux Varietal International Trophy by the Decanter World Wine Awards.

"Big, with quite leafy black fruit and exciting minty perfume. Medium-bodied, supple, graceful and ripe but not flashy. Excellent length and four square tannins," declared the judges at Decanter.

After years of Chinese wine being dismissed as "plonk" by many Western oenophiles, it seems the era of quality Chinese wine is dawning and Li is one of the pioneers.

这酒拥有一种与众不同的优雅，评委们一致打了高分，给了它大奖。绒布一掀开，他们震惊了，这是瓶来自中国宁夏的葡萄酒"加贝兰2009"，酿酒师是拥有留法背景的中国人李德美。他们都对自己的判断产生了惊讶，这不可能，宁夏算是个什么产区，李德美又是谁，听都没听说过。

那一晚，中国葡萄酒在国际比赛上获得历史最好成绩的新闻传到了国内，一片喝彩，从业人员大受鼓舞。但谁也没想到这次得奖很快演变成了一场中国民众和西方媒体之间的激烈口水仗，并一发不可收，升级到了一种小范围的民族情绪的宣泄。

先是法国人按耐不住了，通过媒体声称得奖根本就是弄虚作假，往中国的瓶子里装法国酒。中国是全球第五大葡萄酒消费国，历来是消化法国劣质滞销货的理想市场。要是中国人开始喝自己的酒了，法国酒还怎么卖？

"My life changed after my wine was honored," said Li during an interview with Shanghai Daily early this month when he attended a major Bordeaux wine tasting in the city.

Li is now the consultant winemaker for several wine operations in northern and western China. He lectures in viticulture and wine appreciation at the Beijing University of Agriculture. He's also written a book in Chinese, "Communications from a Chinese Winemaker (2012)."

His third and latest wine, Skyline of Gobi, a red mainly of Merlot grapes, was bottled on January 18, 2013 in the Xinjiang Uygur Autonomous Region in far western China.

After the award, some international wine critics and journalists rushed to contact Li about visiting Chinese vineyards.

One of them, Australian master Andrew Caillard, traveled to the vineyard Li manages, Helan Qing Xue (literally Sunshine and Snow on Helan Mountains), in an isolated desert mountain range on the border of the Ningxia Hui and the Inner Mongolia autonomous regions.

又有其他欧洲媒体跳出来说："这瓶酒的得奖怎么和 Decanter 杂志进驻中国的时间点惊人地巧合？"

此时李德美身在北京，面对各方质疑，格外地平静："这并不意外。在国外待了那么长时间，我早已习惯了中国各行各业在国际上的处境，尤其是起步较晚、处于劣势的行业。若是中国人表现好了，那就被质疑作假，若是表现不好，他们会说，中国人本就如此。"

有些情绪和伤痛可以藏得很深，深到连自己都察觉不到。两年之后伦敦奥运会期间的一则新闻像是一把火点燃了李德美压抑于心中所有的委屈和不满。小将叶诗文为中国游泳队拿下了一枚女子四百米个人混合泳金牌。这枚奖牌颇具象征意义，代表着中国在其传统体育弱项上前进了一大步。西方媒体又开始质疑了，甚至有一记者冲到叶诗文面前质问："你到底有没有服用兴奋剂获得金牌，请你正面回答，有还是没有？"

That's where the award-winning wine was made, a blend of Cabernet Sauvignon, Merlot and Cabernet Gernicht.

Caillard was shooting a new documentary film, "Red Obsession," about the shift in wine consumption power from West to East. Li is depicted as a representative of new Chinese wine production. It is to be released this year.

At the same time, many Western wine media and experts have questioned the superiority of Li's wines and the timing of the award in 2011 to apparently coincide with the launch of the Chinese-language version of Decanter magazine. French wine in Chinese bottles is how some describe Li's efforts.

"Being honored and doubted are both to be expected," Li says, who has now produced three wines in China. The first (a red and a white) in 2003 in a Sino-French demonstration project outside Beijing; the second Jia Bei Lan in Ningxia, and the third Skyline of Gobi. Volume was low in the first two wines. Li hopes Skyline of Gobi, with a larger volume, will be widely distributed and more affordable.

　　"我听了特别愤怒，因为感同身
受。当时被质疑作假的时候，我真
的差点问他：'你是人吗？'但
若真的这样问，使自己陷入口水战
中，不善言辞的我还是忍了。毕竟，
我酿制这款酒既不是为了获奖，更
不是为了跟别人斗个高低。"李德
美说道。

Jia Bei Lan was first produced in 2005 and achieved a high quality in 2008, when it garnered nearly all the awards from Chinese wine associations. The 2009 vintage is even better, according to the vintner. Only 20,000 bottles were produced. It sells for around 800 yuan (US$128) a bottle; that's considered astonishingly high for a Chinese wine, especially given low labor costs.

"I've studied overseas for years, clearly knowing that any outstanding achievement by Chinese, especially in areas where China is not traditionally strong, will be doubted," Li says.

The vintner spent two years in Florida in the United States, studying gardening, and two years in France learning viticulture.

"I have never replied publicly to such doubts since I believe my wine stands the test of time," he says.

"Moreover, such skepticism is inevitable for a New World wine country lacking experience and unrecognized by the Old World during its early stages of development, especially China," Li adds.

这奖，在他看来实至名归，2009 年是宁夏地区极好的年份，用他的话说，这是一个酿酒师的年份。

李德美说，品尝葡萄酒的时刻就像是和酿酒师做一场穿越时空的对话，他和你念叨着那一年里葡萄园发生的故事：那一年的春天很温暖，空气因为下了几场雨的缘故而微微湿润，夏天干燥炎热，冬天却是那么寒冷冗长。那些葡萄藤有的长在迷雾笼罩的山坡上，有的俯身美丽的小河边每天听着流水歌唱。园子里的土壤里布满了深浅不一的碎石。开瓶的那一刻，酿酒师或许正一身泥泞地在葡萄园里挖地、剪枝、收葡萄，抑或许他已离开了这个世界。

"我可以自信地说，那一年（2009）几乎没有犯什么错误，我充分地在这款酒里表达了风土"，李德美说。

尊重风土是李德美酿酒的信念和坚持，也是他的底线。获奖之后，国内外许多酒庄请他去酿酒。

"不管他们出多少钱，我必须拥有管理葡萄园的权力！这就好比一个大厨做菜，他可不是仅仅在厨房的灶台忙活，还要起个大早就去逛菜场，寻觅食材。"李德美对这一点很坚持。

Counted rigorously, China has only 16 years of winemaking experience, he says.

Wine challenge in China

Compared with New World winemakers, such as those in Australia and America, Chinese winemakers face far more difficulties and challenges because of the growing climate.

They may be working the same grapes, but the conditions are very different.

Australian, American and Chilean winemakers are fortunate because they can start by imitating the viticulture mode from Old World wine countries such as France and Spain.

They share similar oceanic climates, warm and dry in the summer (not too hot) and cool and moist in the winter (not too cold).

他称呼那些葡萄为"我的宝贝"，只要有时间就去看看"孩子们"。那些"孩子"要是生了病长了虫，他心疼得要命。伺候他们，一点也不省心。李德美自己都觉得奇怪，要是平常去逛个商场，没走几步就累趴了，可要是在葡萄园里，他能走上一整天！

无论是葡萄酒的老世界产区像是法国、意大利，还是新世界产区比如澳大利亚、新西兰，葡萄之所以能健康地生长很大程度上得益于当地的气候，基本上都是冬暖夏凉，雨热不同季。可是中国却不同，在如此广袤的大地上，却挑不出个完美的生长环境。很多地方夏天又湿又热，容易导致葡萄霉变，冬天又过于干燥寒冷，葡萄不易成熟。宁夏算是相对理想的环境，却也饱受冬季缺雨及不可预测的极寒带来的困扰。

但这不代表中国就出不了伟大的葡萄酒，只是到现在为止，没有找到适应这种气候的种植方式。适应的过程是漫长的，对于全世界都一样，法国用了百年，澳洲、智利则比较幸运，因为气候类似，可以照搬欧洲的经验，只用了几十年。中国可能要更辛苦些，和别人不一样意味着一切从零开始，但对于那份与众不同风土的期待也就更为炙热。

By contrast, China has a distinctive and less-than-ideal climate in many places. Summers can be hot and humid, which easily rot grapes; winters can be too cold and dry. Even in Ningxia, which is comparatively cool, grapes are threatened by over-cold winters and lack of rain in winter, says the winemaker.

"We don't have any experience adapting to the weather, but have had to create our own mode from scratch," says Li.

He spent years developing ways to adapt to Chinese weather, including burying his vines in winter to protect them from cold and digging them out in spring. He still does that.

这十年里，李德美一直在努力探索中国种植模式，该种什么葡萄，怎么种。冬天，他把葡萄藤埋到土里御寒，到了春天再挖出来，这种过冬方式现在被广泛运用。

"我不敢说找到了答案，但这两年在我新项目研究过程中，有了很大的突破。"李德美说道。

"I wouldn't dare to say that I have found way to completely break the limitations of climate, but I have made a big improvement, which is reflected in my latest Skyline of Gobi," he says.

他口中的新项目是新疆天山脚下的天塞酒庄，葡萄园地处古代的丝绸之路上，占地 2000 亩。如果把宁夏的风土比作是个优雅内敛的小姐，那么新疆这块土地上所出产的酒更像是张扬奔放的弗拉明戈女郎。

"宁夏气候温凉，因而产出的酒有着良好的酸度，有时带有白色水果的清新香气；新疆气候干热，夏天光照强，降雨少，若是采收及时，酿出的酒颜色深厚，香气饱满。"李德美解释道。

但他仍然觉得现在给中国的风土下个结论为时过早，对于一个产区特色的归纳需要相当长的种植时间和庞大的产酒基数。要找到个明确的规律和特色，估计还要等上十几年的时间。

所以，他现在只种了 1500 亩葡萄，囊括了美乐、赤霞珠、设拉子、品丽珠、马瑟兰、霞多丽这几个品种。剩下的 500 亩，留着 10 年后种，到那时酒庄已积累了足够的经验，他作为酿酒师也会有新的思考。

李德美如此执着于风土和他早年在法国的留学经历息息相关。

Chinese business people tend to want high returns on short-term investment, but this approach limits the development of the wine industry, which usually needs more than 10 years to recover costs, according to Li.

Respect terroir

After his wine became world-famous, Li has received numerous invitations to make wine at wineries in China and overseas.

"No matter how much wineries pay, I must have freedom to manage the vineyard, which means respecting the terroir," Li says.

Terroir refers to climate, geography, soil and how they affect and interact with each other, giving distinctive characteristics to particular vineyards in particular years.

Li attributes the success of his Jia Bei Lan 2009 to the great vintage, good weather and interplay of many factors.

谁都没想到，这个害羞不起眼的中国人的加入赋予了 Chateau Palmer 那一年份 (2001) 的酒与众不同的意义和额外的价值。Palmer 的这个年份因为李德美的声名鹊起而在中国市场变得格外的紧俏。

记忆回到 2000 年，那年李德美 30 岁。正当人们热闹地迎接千禧年到来，他得到了一个机会去波尔多农业工程师学校学习葡萄酒栽培、酿造和管理。课程为期两年，由法国政府资助，学成归来后效力中法合作的葡萄酒项目——中法庄园。

带着兴奋与期待，李德美踏上了法国这片他向往已久的土地，可没想到迎接他的既不是那香气扑鼻的羊角面包，也不是那浪漫动听的香颂，而是让他抓瞎的法语。

"我当时想着可以用英语对付，人家法国总比我们中国国际化吧，英语总说得比我强啊！没想到波尔多那里更多的是葡萄园农民和产业工人，他们压根不说英语。"李德美回忆道。

"In wine I try to represent all the natural advantages of terroir, while avoiding mistakes during the winemaking process, slightly adjusting the blending and barrel aging according to the climate conditions of a particular year," Li says.

Lu Yang, considered the top sommelier in China and Asia, reads Li's philosophy in his wines.

"I have tasted different vintages of Jia Bei Lan, and they are slightly different. Generally, I get a strong expression of Ningxia terroir from the wine, with the aroma of dried mushroom and herbs," says Lu, now wine director at Shangri-La International Management Group.

Li says the only wineries with which he will cooperate are those that operate their own vineyards and allow the winemaker to be involved in vineyard management.

这意味着他要现学法语，同时还要在限定的时间内拿到学位。法语里有太多需要背的单词和文法，这对于已到而立之年的李德美来说更是困难。他只能白天上课，晚上学语言。凌晨两三点睡觉，六七点起床读书是常态。中国人本来就吃得起苦，于他来说，倒也不算什么。可理论课上完，到了实习阶段，他犯愁了。班上几乎所有的同学都是法国人，靠着自己的人脉和社会关系，很轻易地找到了实习单位。可他呢？学校里唯一的中国人，没有任何背景和基础。眼看着同学一个个都找到了方向，李德美急得像是热锅上的蚂蚁，再加上他个性内敛，也不敢找人帮忙。最后还是导师看出了他的心事，问道："你的实习有问题吗？需要帮助吗？"

在老师的帮助下，李德美成为了Chateau Palmer 的一员，也是酒庄历史上第一个中国员工。

在酒庄里，李德美和同事们相处得格外融洽，有再大的矛盾也不吵架。

"一吵架，我的法语就跟不上了，那我肯定吃亏啊！"他说着，笑了。

"If a winemaker cannot control the original ingredients, the grapes, winemaking will be filled with too many uncertainties and the continuity through vintages cannot be ensured," Li says.

Today Li works in a vineyard covering 133 hectares in Yanqi, also known as Karasahr in central Xinjiang on the Silk Road. He only cultivates 100 hectares of grapes, however, saving the remainder for a time in 10 years or so when he has a deeper and more comprehensive understanding of the terroir, knowing which grape variety suits the soil and climate.

He describes wine reflecting Ningxia terroir as having "good acidity and fresh aroma, some notes of white fruits brought by the cool weather. Xinjiang terroir produces wine with "deep color, rich aroma and intense flavor," he says.

"Respecting nature doesn't mean a loss of my wine personality, which still takes time to cultivate and mature. Although different vintages have differences, there is something subtle, invariable and eternal there. If I capture such subtlety, then my personal style is formed," says the winemaker.

在 Palmer，他"享受"到了这辈子最昂贵的淋浴，到现在回想起来，仍然是又好笑又尴尬。当时他一不小心弄翻了酒桶，鲜红的酒液喷涌而出，把他全身浇了个透。以 Palmer 现在的市场价 2 千多元一瓶来算，一桶那就是十几瓶的量，换算下来那真的是花了几万元洗了次澡呀！那件弄脏了的衣服，李德美到现在还保存着。

实习快结束了，最后那几天，李德美心事重重。他很想问酒庄复印那份工作手册，上面记录着这一年从种植到最终成品的每一个细节，可又不好意思开口，这对于酒庄来说就是商业机密啊！犹豫了几天，他深吸一口气，来到办公室，要求借走那本酿酒操作手册。

"我当时心虚，还特别强调，既然我也参与了工作，或多或少，这本手册的版权也该有我一份吧？"李德美回忆着。

没想到人家特别大方地把手册给了他，还问，去年的、前年的你要不要？一并拿去！

李德美瞬间明白了，被酒庄视为最核心最珍贵的资产并不是酿造技术，而是这块土地所承载的阳光和土壤，也就是 terroir。这是外人拿不走也复制不了的。Chateau Palmer，这个波尔多玛歌地区的三级名庄送别李德美的礼物是 terroir 的真谛。

However, Li's approach differs from that of some French winemakers, says Yao Shangyong, a certified wine taster, who once made wine with Li.

"Unlike many French winemakers throwing themselves into representing terroir without considering the wine drinker, Li balances the terroir with drinkability. After all, not all the characteristics of terroir present in wine are pleasing to many drinkers," says Yao.

2003 年，李德美回国，正式开启了其在国内的酿酒生涯。很多人以为加贝兰是他的第一个作品，其实不然，他的处女作是中法合作项目，位于河北怀来的中法庄园。

按先前的故事看，法国人很清楚授之以鱼不如授之以渔的道理。可是一旦他们来到了中国，怎么就有点鱼渔不分了呢？

为了让这个中法合作项目顺利进行，每隔一段时间法国政府就会派农业专家来庄园指导。高高在上的法国人在中国指着这个说不好，那个说不对。有些在理的，李德美虚心接受，有些不在理的，他对他们说不，还非得辩驳个明白。

法国人很是诧异：你一个学酒没几年的中国人凭什么在我们面前说不？我们可是来自酿酒历史超过百年的国度。

"我当时直截了当地回答，是风土，是我在你们国家学会的这两个字。或许你们比我们更懂种植酿造，但我一个中国人绝对比你们更了解中国的风土！"李德美说到这里，声音更响亮了，不知道是兴奋还是激动。

American, French roots

"Demei's wine presents much Old World style, elegant, implicit and balanced, showing his French roots," says Li Meiyu, sommelier at Park Hyatt Beijing and the winemaker's friend.

But Li Demei's interest in winemaking arose in the New World.

He graduated from China's Northwest Agriculture and Forestry University in Yangling, Shaanxi Province, with a major in gardening. He studied meterology, geology, chemistry, soil, fertilizer, plant biology and other subjects.

At the age of 26, he went to Florida State University Southwest Research Center to continue gardening studies.

"At that time, I only knew that there is a by-product of the grape called wine and I never thought of making wine until one day in my second year in America," Li recalls.

It was November 1997 and he and a friend were driving in northern California when they got lost and found themselves in a vineyard in the Napa Valley.

两段海外的经历，让李德美的酒兼具了新旧世界两种风格，既有法国人那种对于风土的执着，又有美国人以市场化为导向的亲和力，也就是葡萄专业领域所讲的 drinkability，易饮性，往简单里说，就是大众所喜欢的实在味道。

要不是语言的障碍，李德美在法国的日子完全可以过得更滋润些。课堂上所说的那些土壤、肥料、种植、采摘对他来说并不陌生，他本科就在西北农业大学读园艺学，成天研究怎么和泥土种子打交道。

今年 46 岁的他代表着中国特定时代知识分子的命运——被动地接受，没有了自我："我们这个年龄，对于人生，没有太多自己的选择和自由，有学上就不错了。"

大学毕业后，李德美被分配到北京农学院教书，至今他仍然是那里的一名讲师。他开设的葡萄酒品鉴课程是门需要抢注的公共课，因为学长们都说，认真听课认真喝酒就能过！但那是后话了，他一开始教的课程和葡萄酒无关，是本科专业的延续：园艺学。

"I was very impressed. It was an autumn day and all over the hills there were rows of colorful grapes, light yellow, green, golden, pink, red, deep purple. From then on, I started thinking of viticulture and used my camera to capture the vineyard colors," Li says.

Three years later he took part in a two-year Sino-French project in viticulture, oenology and winery management in Bordeaux at the prestigious ENITA (Ecole Nationale D'Ingenieurs Des Travaux Agricoles).

He immersed himself in the French language, often sleeping no more than four hours a night.

He then received an internship at Chateau Palmer, ranked third-growth in Bordeaux, becoming the first Chinese to work there.

初为人师的时候，他才刚过 25 岁，每天讲课研究批作业的生活还是很闷的，时间一长，李德美有些迷茫。学校正好有个和美国佛罗里达大学合作进修的项目，他想去看看外面的世界，寻求些改变。更何况，那是美利坚,那让人向往的美国精神!

在奥斯卡获奖影片《阿甘正传》里，有一句经典台词：在你没有尝到它之前，你永远不知道下一颗巧克力是什么滋味。男主角阿甘借这句话来表达一种美国人所崇尚的生活态度：如果不算上最终的死亡，生命是一场如此精彩却又从来不知道终点在哪里的迷途。既然如此，不如勇敢一点，乐观一点，对未来多一点期待，迷了路，风景或许会更好。

"Palmer was a turning point in my life where I harvested my wine philosophy and winemaking attitude," Li emphasizes. Before ending his internship, he was given permission to copy the working notes on wine growing and winemaking over the years. Staff gave him their own notes.

"The French believe that you can copy their technique but cannot copy their terroir, including the soil and sunshine, which determines their wine," says Li.

In 2003, he returned to China, making his very first wines - one red and one white - in a Sino-French Demonstration Vineyard in Hebei Province. During the process, French winemakers visited and advised. Li frequently challenged the veterans and their advice on how to make wine in China.

They were shocked that a young Chinese winemaker, with only a few years' experience, would question experts with many years experience from a nation with a long winemaking history.

"I answered them without hesitation: 'It's terroir, the most important thing I learned form your country. Although you know more about viticulture, I know more about Chinese terroir'," Li recalls.

Life of a winemaker

"Being a winemaker is boring, hard and lonely but once you fall in love with it, it's also a job you will ever give up until you die," says the vintner.

到美国的那年秋天，学校放假，李德美闲得无聊和朋友一起开车出门，像好莱坞公路电影一样横穿美国大陆。从佛罗里达一路向西，开上了那条最美的一号公路。那条路沿太平洋修建，北起旧金山金门大桥，南接洛杉矶，路的一边是浩瀚无垠的大海，另一边是陡峭高耸的悬崖峭壁，一路上都是各有风情的小镇和国家森林公园。当地人说，在一号公路上开车，就犹如走在天堂的路上。他光顾着看沿途的风景，一不小心走岔了，开进了条蜿蜒小道，越来越窄，也不知道该怎么出去，那个年代，还没有 GPS 导航。开着开着，眼前出现了一片让人窒息的美丽。那是一片蜿蜒起伏的丘陵，上面种满了葡萄树，整整齐齐，一眼望不到边。树上结满了一串串正处转色期的果实，每一颗都有着它自己的颜色，从金黄到那如少女脸颊般的粉红，从浅绿透着点白到深红透着些紫。风飘过的时候，树叶连带着葡萄一起舞动，这感觉就像是奏响一首七彩的热闹的交响乐。后来才知道，那个迷路的地方是美国最知名的葡萄酒产区——纳帕谷。

"在这之前，我就知道葡萄和我接触的其他农产品不同，它非纯农业，而是一种可加工的食物。如果说，那算是隐隐约约地在心头开了扇窗，那么当我看到那片葡萄园的时候，我很清楚地找到了窗户打开的方向。"李德美回忆道。

窗户开了，也便有了之后波尔多的故事。

姚尚勇是李德美曾经的酿酒助理和学生，他对于老师能做到风土和口味两者的平衡和兼顾，很是钦佩："老师虽然在法国学的酿酒，可他并不像许多法国酿酒师那样两耳不闻窗外事埋头于风土，毕竟有许多风土特征，若是真的都通过葡萄酒呈现出来，不仅晦涩难懂，更不惹人喜欢。"

"对于一个酿酒师来说，什么最重要？有人愿意喝你的酒！"李德美如是说。

"我就像是杯 Domaine Chevalier（骑士酒庄），表面上低调，甚至不起眼到容易被人忽略，但这并不影响这酒成为波尔多最顶级的白葡萄酒，因为它又是那么的丰富而深邃。"李德美说。

在我动笔写李老师这篇文章的时候正值 10 月国庆假期，那是北半球葡萄丰收的季节。此时的他正在新疆忙碌着，不是在葡萄园里，就是在酒庄的实验室里。只见 14 个矿泉水瓶子里装着颜色深浅不一的红色液体，砖红、紫红、宝石红一字排开。每个瓶子前面，对应放着个酒杯。李德美仔细地品尝着每一杯的不同，记下密密麻麻的笔记。

很多人以为，酿酒师的生活悠闲惬意，在葡萄园里度过一个又一个浪漫假期，就像是电影《云中漫步》中所描绘的场景：寒冷的冬日，人们在葡萄园里点火生烟，在温暖的篝火映照下，葡萄藤显得没那么尖锐，反倒是更柔和了。可现实中，点火并不是多么让人向往的事情，而是为了抵御寒流的侵袭所作的应急措施。每一场霜冻、冰雹都影响着来年的收成，采收期更像是一场与时间的赛跑。这些都让酿酒师们每天提心吊胆地过日子。

Most of the vineyards in China are in remote and desolate areas where traditional agriculture cannot develop because those crops require different soil types.

"One-third of my time is spent in the vineyard, exposed to the sun and rain, turning over the oil and pruning, just like an ordinary farmer," he says.

There's no room for mistakes. Li checks the smallest detail, from picking the grapes to cleaning the crushers and filters. A decaying grape left inside a vessel can contaminate the wine with bacteria.

"It's also a risky job and even can be life-threatening, so a rigorous working attitude is required," says Yao, the certified wine taster who once made wine with Li.

Li insisted that the carbon dioxide level be tested each time before staff approached the fermentation barrel so they would not be suffocated by carbon dioxide fumes, Yao recalls. "This precaution is neglected by many local Chinese winemakers," he says.

"这份工作辛苦，枯燥而单调，需要强大的定力，耐得住寂寞。等待一年，才出个结果，且不一定是好结果，"李德美感叹。

中国的这些个葡萄园不在上海，不在北京，在荒凉偏僻的山区或是戈壁。白天，他们穿着雨靴和工作服在葡萄园里，灰头土脸，风吹日晒，和农民没什么两样。时不时地，还被农民当成傻子和神经病。农民对于收成的理解局限于有与无，而酿酒师的判断是好与坏。农民们不理解，为什么葡萄熟了，酿酒师决定不采收，却要一等再等。越等风险越大，可是越等，葡萄的成熟度也越高。到了晚上，荒郊野岭的，没有夜生活，甚至连路灯也没有，只有星星作伴，那真是天苍苍，野茫茫，风吹草低见牛羊。李德美只能去觅个好吃的，从他最爱的那碗羊杂汤里得到个慰藉。

Making wine, a living thing that changes and evolves over time, is filled with uncertainties.

"When I'm making wine, I'm not only making its present, but also putting his imagination of its future into the bottle," Li explains.

After the wine is bottled, and it ages with the cork, there is suspense because no one knows how it will taste until the bottle is opened some years later.

Unlike other jobs that can become routine through years of repetition, there is nothing routine about winemaking. "You never slack off for lack of curiosity, because in the world of wine, every day is a new day," Li says.

Some winemakers who are more than 80 years old still visit their vineyards regularly, though they lean on their canes. "I will probably make wine all my life," says Li, "and worry about my wine on my deathbed."

除了耐得住寂寞，酿酒师也是个有生命危险的工作，需要非常细心谨慎。尤其是接近发酵桶的时候，里面发出咕嘟咕嘟冒泡的声音，释放出大量的二氧化碳，足以让人窒息死亡。因为不够仔细而酿成的工作事故在国内外屡见不鲜。

这酒，装瓶的时候是好的，不见得陈年两三年之后，仍然有它的生命力。又或许，历经五年乃至十年，这瓶酒才到达其巅峰状态。很少有人愿意花上十年心力，只为了场充满变数的等待。除非，人们对这份工作有着超越物质的期待。李德美称之为理想，一种融入血液和骨子里的，一辈子的爱。

"我这一辈子呀，合上眼的那一刻都会有遗憾，不知道自己做的酒现在变成了什么样，心被挠得痒痒的。酿酒不会让你满足，因而你永远保持着这份激情。等我老了，可能也会像欧美那些老酿酒师那样颤颤巍巍地拄着拐杖，或是坐在轮椅上，时不时地到葡萄园去看看。"李德美说道。

李老师是山东人，有着北方人的豪爽和热情。只要是和朋友聚会，他经常会带上三瓶酒：加贝兰、天塞和 Chateau Palmer，代表着他从法国到中国一路的改变和成长。可是，他对加州的感情却是深沉而特别的。前不久，他又回了次加州，重访 17 年前因为迷路而偶遇的葡萄园，那是他梦开始的地方。

梦在哪里，未来就在哪里。

Chinese wine production

China is the world's sixth-largest wine-producing country, reaching 135 million 9-liter cases in 2011, ahead of Australia, and is expected to strengthen its position by 2016, according to the industry report by Vinexpo Asia Pacific released this month.

Around 57,000 hectares of vines are cultivated. Wine-growing areas include Shandong, Shanxi and Hebei provinces, the Ningxia Hui Autonomous Region and the Xinjiang Uygur Autonomous Region.

Among which, Shandong is known for its tidal and cinnamon soil and production of Cabernet Sauvignon; Ningxia features a cool climate and sandy soil, producing both red and white grapes such as Merlot, Cabernet Franc and Chardonnay. Xinjiang is known for its Cabernet Sauvignon, Merlot, Syrah, Gamay and Riesling. It is considered by top Chinese winemaker Li Demei as a potential area for producing sweet wine.

Views on Chinese wine

Robert Parker
Influential critic with "a million-dollar nose"

"The Chinese wine I served five years ago was good, but not inspirational. But what I tasted in recent years convinced me that China is a vast country with diverse soils and climates. I think it has a tremendous potential. No matter how good the Chinese wines have become, there will be skeptics."

Jerry Liao
Manager sommelier at Jing An Shangri-La, West Shanghai

"The Chinese wine appellation system is still under an experimenting status, so that thus far there are many inferior wines, either domestically made or imported, labeled with an ambiguous origin. Some Chinese wineries are too volume-oriented to maintain their quality. But I am optimistic that China will be the most potential and dynamic market in the near future."

Steve Spurrier
Consulting editor of Decanter and also organizer of the Judgment of Paris

"I tried an attractive Muscat made in China, very light, clean and aromatic. However, overall, for Chinese wine production, quantity is higher than quality."

Jancis Robinson
British wine critic, international authority and Master of Wine

"I once encountered a wine made from 100-percent Chinese grapes that would surely be an absolutely perfect introduction to wine for anyone such as the more than a billion Chinese who have never so far tasted it. And with its convincing core of fruit, easy grapiness and sizzling crispness, it would be a suitable foil for all manner of mild, spicy, sweet and sticky morsels destined for their chopsticks. Ningxia seems to be the most popular area for the latest round of investment in Chinese vineyards. The climate here is much drier than that of Shandong Province on the east coast, where so many of the first vineyards of the modern era are located."

1. 夏广丽
宁夏夏桐酒庄首席酿酒师

2. 张　静
宁夏贺兰晴雪酒庄首席酿酒师

3. 张军翔
曾长期担任广夏（银川）贺兰山葡萄酿酒有限公司总工程师，现任宁夏大学农学院教授兼大学葡萄酒与葡萄酒教育部工程研究中心副主任

中国杰出酿酒师

香港财神爷

好酒

有道

"从来没有我想要而得不到的酒！"唐英年说得如此自信，甚至有些狂妄，但这也的确符合他亚洲第一红酒收藏家的身份。虽然，他更让人熟知的身份是香港特别行政区政务司前司长，2012 年香港特首候选人。

没人知道唐英年到底有多少瓶酒，多少个秘密酒窖。他自己不愿透露具体数字，但说是最起码几千瓶，多到这辈子都喝不完。这些酒，是对他品味和人生观的折射，从某种意义上说，也是他生活的一种记录。

Asia's
biggest
collector

佳士得曾为唐英年举行过红酒专场拍卖，第一次大规模展现了这位政治家的勃艮第收藏，刷新了单场拍卖的最高成交纪录，622万美金。总共180批次的红酒收藏，囊括了71个酒庄，从1949到2010年共61个年份。其中的6瓶1995年份的大瓶装罗曼尼康帝，被拍到了15000美金，12瓶装的1978年份蒙哈榭以19000美金成交。这些酒的真假，被一些西方媒体质疑，认为如此大规模的顶级佳酿，不可能落入单个收藏家的手中，更何况还是个东方人。

而唐英年的表态是：我就是要通过这场拍卖告诉全世界，亚洲人一样拥有世界级的葡萄酒收藏！佳士得红酒部总监谭耀明这样评价唐的举动：短短十年间，亚洲葡萄酒收藏家已为全球瞩目。他们不仅将最稀有的年份纳入囊中，更是伦敦纽约各大拍卖会上最有力的竞投者。他预计，未来几年内，亚洲买家的国际地位将有进一步提升。

唐英年的办公室在中环置地广场，他的桌上陈列着各种色彩和质地的纺织样品。唐英年也是纺织业巨头唐氏集团的继承人。富家公子的形象让人相信，唐英年收藏大规模的顶级佳酿，自然有其财务保证。

In the wine world, former Hong Kong politician Henry Tang is a larger-than-life wine collector; in Hong Kong he is revered as a teacher, a master, even a god. He talks to Ruby Gao.

Former Hong Kong politician Henry Tang is arguably the biggest wine collector in the world and almost certainly the biggest in Asia. Among wine collectors, he has been described as larger than life, and in Hong Kong he is sometimes called sifu (师傅), Cantonese for master, or even caiye (财爷), the God of Wealth.

对于大自然与酒之间的微妙联系，唐英年充满了好奇，为此一次次地飞到法国葡萄园里去寻找答案。渐渐地，他也养成了习惯，在做出买酒决定之前，去一次产酒的葡萄园，亲身感受酒的风土。

唐英年坦陈买酒需要很多钱，但若是提升到收藏的境界，钱的作用是有限的，贵的不见得是好的，有钱也不一定买得到想要的。他认为，好的酒是诚实的，毫无保留地诉说着它从哪里来，酿酒师付出的心，甚至葡萄收获的那一年有多少个晴天。举例来说，那些老酒倒入杯中，其边缘便会呈现一圈橘色的光晕，那是岁月的痕迹；勃艮第产区的酒就是有股优雅的花香；而波尔多的酒一定会透着那份摄人心魄的阳刚。他一点也不喜欢那些人为痕迹明显，所谓完美，贵到咋舌的酒，太做作。这解释了在他的收藏里，既有罗曼尼康帝这种号称世界上最昂贵的酒，也有 Simon Bize 这种在欧洲售价才 30 欧的酒款。

葡萄酒是靠天吃饭的行业，若是碰到一个糟糕的年份，多下了几场雨，无论酿酒师再怎么努力，酒都不会好喝，也就失去了其市场价值。很多收藏家尽可能地搜罗年份好，产量稀有的名庄酒，这些酒的增值空间是难以估量的。唐英年却经常是好年份坏年份照单全收。

While in government, he was instrumental in helping make Hong Kong Asia's wine hub when he abolished import duties on wine in 2008. By 2010, more wine was being sold in Hong Kong auctions than in London and New York, the traditional wine trading centers. The Chinese mainland still charges import duty.

The former Hong Kong chief secretary for administration lost his bid in 2012 to become the Hong Kong Chief Executive.

Hong Kong-born Tang, 61, has spent more than 30 years collecting wine. He was born into a family in the textile industry and has been involved in business and many aspects of government for many years.

Despite all his resources, Tang says money alone is not enough to become a successful wine collector. It takes passion for appreciating wine that stands the test of time and a commitment to his own wine aesthetics, which he describes as the expression of terroir.

"这是出于对酿酒师的尊重。无论是好年份还是坏年份，他们投入的心血是一样的。"唐英年不经意间对我说的这句话，让人动容。如此的不功利让他获得了众多酒庄和酿酒师们的尊重，他们总会把最好的酒留给他。唐英年最喜爱的酿酒师是 Henri Jayer。这位法国酿酒师会在好年份酿出令人惊叹的作品，而在坏年份仍然保持住一定的水准。从上世纪 80 年代到 2006 年 Jayer 去世，唐英年坚持每一年都买入一定数量，那是迄今为止他自认最伟大的收藏。他几度飞到法国，就为了和 Jayer 分享品酒心得。

"So far, there hasn't been any wine that I desire but have been unable to acquire," Tang told Shanghai Daily in a face-to-face interview in Hong Kong late last month.

Tang compares himself to a glass of pinot noir, saying both he and the wine have "finesse, character and elegance."

Tang recently made headlines when part of his Burgundy collection went under the hammer at Hong Kong Christie's auction on March 16 and fetched US$6.22 million. The 810 lots included wine from 71 Burgundy producers, their vintages ranging from 1949 to 2010. Six magnums of Romanée-Conti 1995 were sold for HK$1,210,000 (US$156,695). Twelve bottles of Montrachet 1978 were sold for HK$847,000.

"It is the first single-owner Asian collector sale," says Simon Tam, Christie's head of wine in China.

"I realized I have far too much wine, and I would never be able to consume it in a lifetime. So I decided to present a selection of wines at auction, and provide wine lovers around the world with the opportunity to purchase great bottles and enjoy the journey. After all, the best wines are those shared," says Tang.

"I also hope to tell the world through this auction that Westerners are not the only wine lovers with major collections - Asians too have world-class collections," he adds.

James Suckling是全球最负盛名的酒评家之一。他回忆道，"Henry 很多时候扮演着一个老师的角色，他总能启发引导我们去捕捉和体验葡萄酒细腻到让人容易错过的美。"

香港的葡萄酒业内人士都爱称呼唐英年为师傅。一来是因为他藏酒 30 年，喝的比谁都多，拥有着难以企及的品酒功力，二来他作为一个长者，对后辈和朋友非常的慷慨。

唐英年对自己的品酒能力颇为自信，分享了自己在法国一家餐厅的经验。当时，他点了瓶很昂贵的酒。法国侍酒师拿来一瓶坏掉的酒，想在眼前这张东方面孔前蒙混过关。结果可想而知，那个法国人为此付出了赔偿一瓶的代价。"目前还没有哪瓶酒能逃过我的鼻子。"唐英年说到这件事，显得很是得意。

对酒的选择，他向来不受外界因素干扰，只相信自己的味蕾判断。比如，在 30 年前，一个没人听说过的新酒庄 Le Pin 把它 1982 年产的酒卖到了 600 镑一箱，当时一箱木桐庄（五大名庄之一）才 300 镑。他一喝，视其为沧海遗珠，毅然买了好几箱。今日，这款酒，即使是花 6 万镑，也不一定买得到。

Tam, from Christie's, agrees.

"In a short 10 years, Asian collectors learned a lot about wine and have amassed very fine collections quickly. They are a major force, not only in wine auctions in Hong Kong, but also in international auctions outside of the region," Tam tells Shanghai Daily.

Today they stand as an important buying group in each of Christie's sales in New York and London, he adds. "Buyers will become more discerning and concentrate on only the top wines with the best storage and provenance. We forecast increased demand for rarer and more difficult-to-source vintages in Asia."

Although Tang declines to disclose the size of his collection, he does say that the base of the collection is "at least thousands of bottles with both old and new vintages covering the five First Growth chateaux and Burgundy wines."

他的自信和骄傲在佳士得为他举行的红酒专场拍卖会上受到了公然的挑衅。他的一款 1959 罗曼尼康帝和 1978 蒙哈榭被西方媒体质疑是假酒。平时一脸笑容的师傅没有了好脾气，甚至以诽谤罪对质疑者进行起诉。"如果买新酒，我会直接从酒庄购进，或是 en primeur（期酒）。对于老酒，我都会追溯其出处，详细到它被经手的每一任买主，被存放过的每一个仓库。买到假酒的可能性，几乎是可以排除的。"唐英年强调。

师傅的大方是出了名的，他一直奉行独乐不如众乐的原则。在担任香港财政司司长期间，他曾带领香港电影代表团参加戛纳影展，当场打开好几瓶珍藏的 1983 年份 Petrus 招待媒体。在香港，要是被受邀参加唐英年的酒局，那比中六合彩还要令人兴奋，因为他一定会拿出最好的酒，并为之配上顶级的佳肴。他的最爱是牛排配赤霞珠，披萨配意大利 Barbaresco，还有黑品诺，于他看来，可以和所有的食物完美共存。师傅觉得，这世间最美好的事情莫过于分享。

World-class collectors need to demonstrate that they have more than 20 vintages to prove their quality, and the wine needs to be cellared in a perfect condition, says Tam.

Tang has told the Wall Street Journal that his wines are housed in his various cellars around the world. "I have received many wine-related propositions, from buying wineries and vineyards to selling the wine collection, and I refused all of them. Wine is my person interest. It is impossible for me to enjoy it fully when it becomes a business."

Wine aesthetics

Tang's recent wine auction reflects his personal taste, which is diverse and eclectic, says James Suckling, former European bureau chief of Wine Spectator magazine, and a friend of Tang's for more than 10 years.

"The wines sold at the auction feature a wide range of Burgundy, ranging from top-level Grand Cru to village level, from renowned Domaines to lesser-known up-and-coming producers," says Tam from Christie's.

香港的普通百姓不怎么叫唐英年师傅，而喜欢称呼他财爷，不仅因为他担任过香港财政司司长，更因为他发起并促成了特区政府2008年对于葡萄酒关税的废除。这使得如今的香港超越了纽约和伦敦，一跃成为了全球最大的红酒交易中心。

唐英年评价他当年的举措："其实，我的初衷是创造更多的就业机会来增加香港的经济活力。我的目标也达成了，零关税政策为香港创造了最少5000个新岗位，涉及拍卖、物流、展览、餐饮、贸易等等行业。"但是，财爷觉得自己的作用是有限的，零关税的成功更大程度上得益于香港的先天优势，尤其是先进的物流管理，发达便捷的交通以及对于外来文化固有的开放与包容。

人们不免拿上海和香港作比较。大陆的一些葡萄酒业内人士认为上海会成为继香港之后的第二个葡萄酒中心。财爷对此持保留态度，认为上海最起码要满足三个条件：首先是改变内地现有的关税制度。不然，对于葡萄酒的进口价格和种类，上海都不存在任何优势。其次是文化。在他眼中，上海已然是大陆葡萄酒文化最成熟的市场，但这是相对的。要做到真正意义上的成熟，上海还有着很长的一段路要走。最后是品质。对于高品质的酒，大陆没有足够好的储存设备。假酒问题依然没有解决。

"My wine aesthetics is that good wine is not necessarily expensive but reflects the terroir honestly and naturally, and that's why I love Burgundy," Tang says. "In this wine-growing area, there are many winemakers with passion and dedication making wine that best expresses terroir."

"A good wine has its natural color and aroma reflecting its vintage and terroir. Old wine has its distinct color with an orange tint. Burgundy wine has its due floral note, while Bordeaux wine distinguishes itself through its masculine character," Tang explains.

Tang doesn't like wines produced by winemakers who rely on various post-production techniques to make the so-called perfect wine.

He often visits French vineyards, observing operations and studying the soil, one of the key components of terroir, before deciding on a purchase.

Tang says he's not surprised that wines from big-name wineries such as Domaine de la Romanée-Conti and Henry Jayer sell at record prices no matter who the collector is since they have their market price.

He is impressed, however, by some inexpensive wines. For example, Simon Bize from France is usually sold in Europe at 30 euros (US$39) a bottle, but it is sold at the auction for 80 euros, indicating that buyers are willing to pay a premium for wines that he himself appreciates.

Collecting strategy

Many people collect wine for investment and many collect to demonstrate their wealth, status and taste. Of course, many also collect because they love wine.

Tang says he collects wine purely for drinking, which partly explains his approach to collecting which is relatively less speculative than other collectors.

"I don't do vertical collection intentionally because I respect the idea of optimal drinking," says Tang.

A vertical collection is composed of several consecutive vintages of the same wine. For example, a vertical of Romanée-Conti may include a bottle of each vintage from 1990 through 1995.

Older wine is not necessarily better and Tang says wine should be consumed when it's optimal. Simon Bize, for example, is not suitable for long storage, according to Tang.

"However, last week, I tasted a bottle of Romanée-Conti La Tache 1962. The wine, although old, smells florally, tastes pure and lively," he says.

"I also collect both good and bad vintages out of respect for winemakers," Tang says further of his strategy.

Whether it's a good year with perfect sunshine and rainfall or a bad year, winemakers put the same dedication and commitment into their wine, Tang explains.

Henri Jayer (1922-2006) is a vintner Tang holds in highest regard. He has bought his wine every year consecutively since the 1980s. Tang has visited the Jayer winery and talked with him many times. He calls Jayer a Burgundy master who can make outstanding wine in a good year and maintain his wine at a certain level in a bad year.

Tang considers his collection of Henri Jayer his greatest achievement.

His collecting strategy clearly contributes to good relations with various chosen wineries. An essential principle with Tang is provenance: the verified history of a wine's geographic origins, its chronology of storage and ownership.

Provenance includes the assessment of the liquid and is extremely important when it comes to older vintages and guarding against wine fraud.

"Buying a firsthand wine, especially en primeur (buying wines early when they are still in the barrel) is undoubtedly safe because I know how it's born, bottled and shifted to my desk, in detail. However, if I buy an old wine, verifying provenance is the most important thing," says Tang.

Respected wine sifu

Tang buys his wines from an auction house, directly from known wineries and reliable collectors whom he has known for many years. To verify provenance, he checks every detail, including geographic origin and how the wine is cellared.

The authenticity of some of Tang's wines on the auction list is doubted by some wine insiders, including three bottles of 1959 Romanée-Conti and a case of 1978 Romanée-Conti Montrachet.

"My focusing on provenance can virtually eliminate the possibility of buying fake wine," Tang says.

Some collectors, critics and wine lovers in Hong Kong call Tang sifu, a Cantonese expression meaning teacher and master, showing regard for his knowledge acquired through 30 years of collecting and tasting.

"He really is like a teacher in many ways, and Henry likes nothing better than discussing the details of wine, from production to flavor profiles. The sifu always enlightens everyone about the subtleties of the wine experience," Suckling, formerly with Wine Spectator, writes in his blog.

"Very often, when I dine in a restaurant in France, the sommelier tries to serve me the bottle, which is not corked, and there's something wrong though it's usually hard to discern. But they never succeed and escape from my tasting," the sifu says.

Tang is also held in respect because of his generosity, often sharing his wine collection with friends.

Suckling recalls that Tang and he attended the Cannes Film Festival when Tang was Hong Kong's chief secretary and wanted to promote Hong Kong's film industry.

"He poured magnums of 1983 Petrus to the two dozen press members attending! They were all from his private cellar in London," Suckling recalls.

"I love sharing, that's why I prefer collecting the outsized bottle," Tang says.

Tang enjoys holding wine dinners with friends. "I don't like drinking wine by itself. Wine is intrinsically linked with food from the time it was born."

Besides collecting wine, Tang is also known as a food connoisseur. Steak with Cabernet Sauvignon and pizza with Barbaresco are among his favorite pairings.

"But the perfect pairing for me is Burgundy pinot noir with any food. The wine is so versatile," says Tang.

"I would not dare call myself sifu but I do introduce wine culture to my friends a lot," he adds.

Before losing the election in 2012, Tang had been Hong Kong's chief secretary for four years and had spent at least six years in other government positions. While in government, Tang had to sacrifice some of his passion for wine to serve the public interest.

Before 2002, when he first joined government, he visited Burgundy once a year, but during a decade in public office, he says he visited Burgundy only once. After leaving government last year, he has visited his beloved wine-growing region three times.

Cutting import duty

Slashing Hong Kong's wine duty to zero is recognized one of Tang's major contributions to Hong Kong's development.

Tang initiated the duty-free policy by first halving it in 2007, and later the new Financial Secretary John Tsang completed it by reducing the other half.

Hong Kong started to abolish all taxes on wine imports in 2008, spurring a boom in the wine trade. Today Hong Kong surpasses New York and London as a wine auction hub.

"My original intention was to create more jobs by injecting economic vitality," he says.

He quotes statistics to show that the no-tariff policy created 5,000 new jobs directly related to wine auctions, logistics, exhibitions, hospitality and trade industries. Many other new jobs are indirectly related to wine trade.

Some Hong Kong locals call him the "Wine Caiye."

According to Tang, advanced logistics management, convenient transportation and open attitudes toward Western culture have contributed to Hong Kong's rise in the wine world.

Shanghai has the potential to become a second Hong Kong in Asian wine trade, he says, but it has some significant limitations - tax, culture and ensuring authenticity.

"First is the regulation. Complicated tariffs prevent Shanghai people from sourcing wine freely from all over the world," Tang says.

"Second is the culture. Although in the past five years, the wine culture in Shanghai has developed much faster than Hong Kong which already appreciates wine culture, it takes time to mature."

"Third is the quality. Shanghai's wine storage has room for improvement. Guaranteeing wine authenticity is still a big challenge for the city," Tang says.

Q & A

Q: Were there some value surprises in your collecting?

A: It's my collection of Le Pin 1982. During the 1980s, a wine dealer who knew my taste, often introduced me to some newcomers, including Le Pin, a young unknown winery established in 1979 in Bordeaux.

I was shocked at the price 600 British pounds (US$927.26) a case. At that time, a case of Chateau Mouton (First Growth Bordeaux) cost around 300 British pounds per case. I was impressed by the taste and bought several cases.

Today, Le Pin has become one of the most sought-after and expensive wines and its 1982 vintage is said to be the best with very few production, 300 cases. It's hard to source one case even if you are willing to pay 60,000 British pounds.

I am not just surprised but also inspired. Successful collection is based on being confident in my own wine taste.

Q: Do you recall an embarrassing moment in collecting?

A: It happened during the 1990s. Aubert de Villaine, owner of Domaine de la Romanée-Conti, showed me around Vosne Romanee Village, pointing out which vineyard makes Romanée-Conti, which one produces La Tache. When we crossed a small vineyard, only around a hectare, he kept silent. Later he said the vineyard La Grande Rue, and did not belong to Domaine de la Romanée-Conti. Production is low and the quality is not very good.

I thought that if the vineyard is surrounded by other vineyards producing top wines, then its terroir should not be too bad. And maybe Villaine wasn't candid since it wasn't his vineyard. I insisted on buying a parcel and found that he was totally correct. The taste is not good. I still have most of them.

Q: How did your interest in wine begin?

A: My interest in wine started with curiosity. Forty years ago, I studied at Michigan University in the United States, where beer and whisky are popular. I don't like either, calling them gui lao liang cha 鬼佬涼茶 (literally "Westerners' herbal tea"). I turned to wine and soon became curious about why a bottle of French Cabernet can be 100 times more expensive than a Cabernet made elsewhere. I looked for answers in the library but failed. I was inspired when I became friends with a wine shop owner.

Q: What's the next wine collecting trend?

A: I think wine collecting will turn back to old Bordeaux wines. In the past few years, new wine collectors prefer buying cases of new Bordeaux wines to satisfy their demand for quantity, which pushes up the price. However, old Bordeaux wines, sold by the bottle, haven't won their favor, so prices remain reasonable.

Q: Is there a wine that especially touches your heart?

A: I tasted a bottle of 1947 Cheval Blanc during the 1970s, when I finished my studying in the US and came back to Hong Kong. I was deeply impressed. How could a Bordeaux wine be so rich yet balanced?

国内第一"少庄主"的
奔跑人生

陈芳,怡园酒庄创始人陈进强先生的长女,毕业于美国密歇根大学,取得心理学、妇女学学位;2002年起任怡园酒庄董事长。

怡园的故事,是关于寻根与传承的诉说,是一场历时两百年的长跑。

Winemaking:
a family affair

这两年，庄主陈芳被葡萄酒磨出了耐性，爱上了跑马拉松。只要是在酒庄，她定会起个大早，绕着葡萄园跑上一大圈。她在前面跑着，园里的一条小白狗在后面呼哧呼哧地吐着舌头紧紧跟着。

"跑步是真的很闷。这甚至是一样使人精神分裂的活动。跑的过程中，最少有三个人——你自己、天使和魔鬼。天使当然是沿途鼓励你，但同时你亦会听见魔鬼的冷嘲热讽。偶尔还会灵魂出窍，看着不停被天使和魔鬼缠绕的自己。"陈芳说道。

但沿途的风景是真的很美。她的葡萄园位于山西省的太谷县，占地200公顷，距离太原约40公里的距离。这其中有一条深幽的小路，是她的最爱。路很窄，两旁种着成排的赤霞珠、设拉子、马瑟兰，还有山西的特产——枣子树。成群的鸟儿常会循着葡萄的香气飞来，叽叽喳喳的。一路跑到底，直到没了路，前方是悬崖峭壁，山被大自然的鬼斧神工切成了一片一片，露出了土黄色的岩壁，纹理平滑而清晰，视野也随之开阔起来。

陈芳这时想起了祖奶奶的一句话："如果回家，走到没了路，就是家。"这话透着一股漂泊的凄凉。从她祖辈开始，"漂泊"二字就是人生的主题。

她的祖父是福建龙岩人，13岁离家去南洋讨生活。她的父亲，怡园的创始人陈进强1951年出生于印尼棉兰，后又回北京读书，去内蒙古插队，在呼和浩特当过工人，又转去太原工学院读书，最后辗转到香港做外贸进出口。

厌倦了这样的颠沛流离，陈进强有强烈的愿望想寻回他的根。葡萄藤是最爱往地里钻的，越是贫瘠的土地，越是拼命地扎根去吸收地下的养分，根越来越深，越来越牢，直到自己成为这片土地的一部分。

"其实，我们没有根的人，更想扎根。对于我们来说，做葡萄酒更吸引我们的不是赚钱，不是品牌，是根。陈芳说的时候，下意识地突出"根"的发音。

1997 年，陈进强把根扎在了山西这片故土，种下了第一株葡萄树。中国从此诞生了第一个家族经营酒庄——怡园。陈芳很钦佩父亲在亚洲金融风暴席卷香港的时候，依然投身一个完全不熟悉的领域："我不能说他有远见，但他肯定是勇敢的。"

选地的过程，颇番周折。陈进强回忆道，当年他和法国葡萄酒专家 Denis Boubals 教授开着车，跑遍了山西和陕西。当时的交通不比今日，没有高速公路，全是泥泞的小路。他们去过清徐县，那里都是坡地，是中国历史悠久的葡萄产区，可是工业污染太厉害。他们也去过乔家大院附近，但那里已没有了那份大自然的淳朴和安静。最终，在太古县，教授挖起脚下的一把土，放在嘴边（听说是尝了尝），定下了酒庄的位置，种下了时至今日怡园最重要的五大葡萄品种：赤霞珠、美乐、品丽珠、霞多丽、白诗南。

When she was just 24, Judy Leissner took over her family business, Grace Vineyard, in a village in Shanxi Province. She tells Ruby Gao the story of China's first family-owned winery.

Judy Leissner, president of Grace Vineyard, compares herself to a glass of Champagne, vibrant with good acidity while young and showing distinctive charm with age.

"More importantly, its bubbling character echoes my talkative and sociable personality, befitting the wine industry. A big role of a vineyard owner is telling the story of her wine, which gives it value beyond the bottle," 36-year-old Leissner tells Shanghai Daily in an interview at her wine shop in the city.

Grace Vineyard is the first family-owned vineyard in China and is known for high-quality, affordable "boutique" wine.

此时的陈芳还是那个 Judy Chan，在美国密歇根大学攻读心理学和非常冷门的女权学。毕业后，她加入了香港的投资银行高盛，在人力资源部工作。

那一年，陈芳 24 岁。陈进强把她叫到办公室："我在山西有个葡萄园，你去接手吧。"

"什么？你竟然有个葡萄园？！我对这个完全不懂，你要是早点告诉我，我还能进修下相关课程。那我从最基础的工作开始吧！"陈芳大吃一惊。

"我是要培养你成为创业者，而非职业经理人，这一点你应该明白！"陈进强回答。

A wall in Leissner's Shanghai wine shop is covered with her family photos, documenting the family firm and featuring her father, the founder, her husband, two daughters and herself.

"Here I can receive the real feedback from customers, unlike the more polished feedback from restaurants and hotels that serve my wine," says the US-educated vintner, who is based in Hong Kong.

Grace Vineyard (Yi Yuan, meaning Elegant and Beautiful Vineyard) was established by Leissner's father, Chinese-Indonesian Chan Chun Keung, 16 years ago in Shanxi Province. Leissner took over her father's business when she was only 24 years old.

The vineyard was recognized internationally in 2008 when its 2005 Chairman's Reserve Cabernet Sauvignon received the Decanter World Wine Award.

Today there are more quality Chinese wineries such as Silver Heights and Jade Valley, but Grace is generally considered the first strong statement that made-in-China wine can mean quality. Grace is one of the few labels providing Chinese access to affordable fine wine.

Decanter said: "Judy Leissner ... (is) making unarguably the top wines in China and likely to spearhead any Chinese move to fine wine."

Last year, Leissner became the first recipient of the Asian Wine Personality award from the Institute of Master of Wine. She was honored for promoting wine in Asia through winemaking, marketing and sales.

"Although I visit the vineyard
in Shanxi once a month,
I spend most of my time
flying around the world
to tell the story of Grace
Vineyard," says Leissner.

It's a story of inheritance.

Grace Vineyard covers 200 hectares in Taigu Village in the middle of coal-rich Shanxi. It has sandy soil and a continental climate. Five main grape varieties, three red and two white, are planted — Cabernet Sauvignon, Merlot, Cabernet Franc, white Chardonnay and Chenin Blanc.

陈芳不明白。但她从小就习惯了父亲不按常理出牌的个性。刮台风了，父亲偏偏带着她和弟弟到海边看海浪，感受自然的威力。他还曾带着她一天跑三个电影院看了三部电影。后来，怡园请桃乐丝先生（后来成为怡园的经销商）吃饭，人家事先打招呼说不能吃辣，他却因为自己爱吃辣，叫了一桌子辣菜。结果客人吃得满脸通红，满头大汗。陈芳崇拜父亲，从小向往有一天能和他一起工作。她答应了，从此人生有了戏剧性的改变。可是，她雷厉风行的作风在黄土高坡遇上了一个又一个软钉子。

在香港，加班是家常便饭，一天24小时永远都不够用。可在山西，当地人一到中午就哈欠连天，午睡两小时是生活习惯。开个会，没一小时闲聊绝对不进入正题。酒庄的老员工们只听老庄主的话，根本不把她放在眼里。当时国语不怎么流利的她还要和一口山西口音的政府官员打交道。

逐渐适应之后，陈芳倒享受起反差带来的趣味。尤其是每年冬天，她早上还在充满热带风光的香港，下午就坐飞机赶到了雪花飘飘的北方。

Leissner's father's choice of Shanxi for a vineyard was questioned by many wine experts because the province is highly polluted and contains many coal mines and factories.

Chan, the retired founder, ran a coal mining business in Shanxi for many years.

He recently said, "I felt it was my duty to make up for the damage that had been done to the environment."

In explaining his choice of location, he emphasized that it is in the central basin, far from the northern and southern areas where the mining industries are concentrated.

There's another family history reason behind the location, Leissner says.

"My family, from my grand-father to father, led a wandering life filled with turbulence, roving from nan yang (Southeast Asia 南洋) to China's mainland and then to Hong Kong when the 'cultural revolution' (1966-76) happened. We have a strong intention to sink our roots for a stable life and legacy that can be passed on, Wine fits," she says.

陈芳成为少庄主不久，怡园迎来了其第一个（2001）和第二个（2002）酿酒年份。那两年天气温暖，阳光充沛，采收的葡萄质量让人满意，酿出的酒色泽漂亮，酒体圆润，结构饱满，余味悠长，产量高达100万瓶。少庄主万万没想到，等待她的竟是一场大考验。用她自己的话来说，是 disaster！

山西因为煤矿污染严重，在中国市场上的形象受重挫。而家族式精品酒庄的概念，被多数国人解读为"不上档次的小品牌"。100万瓶好酒，怡园一共才卖掉2万瓶，剩下的98万瓶全都积压在仓库里。日子一天天过去，酒庄一天天亏钱。终于，陈芳忍痛下了一个决定，砍掉葡萄园里一半的葡萄树以控制下一年的产量，减少库存压力。当时，陈芳手里掌管的除了葡萄园，还有父亲位于江西的陵园。

"从醉生到梦死，我都做齐了。做墓园可比葡萄酒容易多了，最起码不用看老天的脸色。"陈芳说。

Leissner attributes the success of Grace Vineyard to her faithfully following her family's core value: a jiefang (街坊) business. Jiefang literally means neighbor and refers to a small, long-time business that targets nearby residents and relies on word-of-mouth marketing.

"Sellers cannot be too ambitious and profit-driven or it's impossible for their products to be worth the price. I can expand the production and raise the price but am not willing to," says the young entrepreneur. "For me, customers becoming friends is more important than making money. That may sound like a fairy tale that many people don't believe but I do think that way."

According to Leissner, most customers see wine as one way of accessing a Westernized, somewhat romantic, lifestyle. She says customers would be angry if they discovered they were stupidly paying for an overpriced bottle.

That approach led to her two major business decisions, which she considers her best and most far-reaching in the past 11 years.

In 2004, after launching the first and second vintages, Leissner decided to remove half the vines and slash production because they were losing money.

The first vintage was a disaster: A million bottles were produced but only 20,000 were sold. Part of the reason was Shanxi's reputation for pollution. Also, the concept of a "boutique" business does not convey the all-important idea of cachet and status to many Chinese.

"It was impossible to keep the brand value and quality distribution under this kind of inventory pressure," Leissner says. "Although the sales increased two years later and all the vines were replanted, I do not regret having made that choice."

In 2007, heavy rainfall seriously damages the quality of the grape. She determined not to make a reserve wine, only premium and table wine.

Their wine was out of stock in 2008. Any of the 2007 vintage, if labeled reserve, would have been sold, but she refused.

"If I could turn back, I wouldn't make any wine that year!" she says.

2007 年的春夏，光照，温度，一切都是那么完美，葡萄园里的人都开始美美地憧憬一个好年份。可到了 9 月，山西竟遭遇了当地十年不遇的大雨，整整下了 15 天！浇灭了陈芳和她的酿酒师所有的期待。没有健康的葡萄，自然产不了好酒。陈芳做出了个让周边人咋舌的决定：停产其高端珍藏系列，只做中档及普通餐酒。当时，谁也没想到这是黎明前的黑暗。

隔年，怡园的 2005 年份赤霞珠庄主珍藏荣获了 Decanter 大奖，重新唤起了全球包括 Jancis Robinson 在内的酒评家对中国这块风土的注意。"中国葡萄酒"这五个字开始被赋予了新的定义。西方社会慢慢打破对这五个字曾经的固有印象："劣质"、"勾兑"、"假拉菲"。

得了奖，怡园的酒瞬间卖断了货。有人建议陈芳把 2007 年的普通餐酒贴上珍藏系列的标，保准贴一瓶，卖一瓶。

陈芳拒绝了："要是我能回到过去，那年我一瓶都不做！"

Heritage of innovation

"In Europe, people can watch over their family business even as they cling to old, traditional ways. But in fast-paced China, you cannot survive without innovation; heritage and 'legacy' are not enough," Leissner says.

As an entrepreneur, she's not conservative and top-down but innovative and open-minded.

"My winemaker from Malaysia has a wine aesthetic totally different from mine. He loves Napa style, rich and bodied, while I prefer the Old World, Burgundy style, elegant. I allow him to make a small portion that he likes but always remind him not to kidnap the whole winery," says the vineyard owner.

Leissner is dedicated to experimenting — from grape varieties and terroir to new ways of dealing with farmers and team building. Leissner is now growing a small area of Riesling, Pinot Noir, Shiraz, Marselan and Aglianico.

"我们是做街坊生意的，这是怡园的核心价值，也是我们的初心。"陈芳解释道。

她开始明白父亲当年的苦心。身为职业经理人，看的是短期的利益，钱不赚不做，有风险不做。唯有创业者，才敢于去冒险，甚至为了长远的利益去承受眼前的失败。

得奖后的怡园势如破竹，口碑和销量一年比一年好，往夸张里讲，改写了中国的高端餐饮业。曾经，在香格里拉、凯悦这样的五星级酒店，或是像 Jean Georges 这样米其林三星厨师开的高档餐厅里，酒单上是没有中国产区这一栏的，因为质量太差。怡园的出现，让这些酒单厚了，多出了一页，上面写着"中国"。这几年里中国那一栏，越来越长，继山西怡园之后，宁夏的银色高地、陕西的玉川酒庄异军突起。要是带着外国朋友去用餐，点一瓶这样的酒已成为一种文化自信的彰显，且一定会加一句："This is Chinese terroir."（这是属于中国的风土）加上怡园的酒售价合理，中高端的也就 300 元左右，这使得他们在市场上一直处于供不应求的状态。形势如此之好，陈芳依然不愿意增产也不愿提价，坚持做自己的"街坊生意"。

In 2011, she established her second vineyard in Ningxia Hui Autonomous Region, finding that the Cabernet grapes grown there has a fruitier taste and deeper color than the wine from Shanxi. A winery there is under construction; the main winery is in Shanxi.

"It's still too early to tell which areas and grapes are best for Chinese winemaking. Making wine is not as romantic as we imagine but scientifically based on plenty of rigorous experiments," she says.

Leissner once invited local grape farmers to a wine tasting.

"But that proved to be the worst decision. They disliked tannic and balanced wine," she explains, adding that they prefer sweeter wine.

She's now thinking of giving up cooperation with local farmers and growing vines with her own trained employees.

街坊生意的特征就是不贵且不差，利润虽不厚，但生命力顽强。在中国的南方，有很多这样背景的百年老店，做的都是熟客，没有营销，靠的就是口口相传。于葡萄酒来说，扩大产量和提升品质基本上是相矛盾的，虽然这并不绝对。全球范围内，最昂贵的酒，像是罗曼尼康帝，一年才几千瓶。在葡萄园里，有经验的果农会秉承优生优育，刻意控制果实数量来确保有限的养分和光照都集中在少数的葡萄里，让它们够浓郁。

"如果我真的提价了，消费者尝了之后发现并不值，那么我就永远失去他们了。我觉得和客人交朋友比赚钱更重要。"陈芳说。

少庄主一边坚守着初心，一边承受着中国的葡萄酒之重。她说道，在本来就已崇洋媚外到极致的中国精品酒市场，本国的生产商承受着比进口商更沉重的税收负担。葡萄园到底是属于国家还是庄主自己，也一直没有个答案。酿酒这块，陈芳和她的酿酒师也仍在摸索，并没有找到任何可遵循的规律。

"Even if we guarantee their income and a bonus if the sugar and acidity are particularly high, they are not dedicated but money-driven. Their focus on vines is not persistent but depends on the market performance," according to the vintner.

Sometimes it makes more economic sense to them to grow other crops.

Leissner is also rebuilding her own professional team, because she faces the challenge of customers more knowledgeable than staff.

Leissner was put in charge of the vineyard when she was only 24, and had settled into her first job as an HR analyst at Goldman Sachs. She was a fresh graduate from the University of Michigan, majoring in psychology and women's studies. She didn't know that her father owned a vineyard. She didn't drink at all back then and knew nothing about wine, management or the Chinese market.

"I asked to work from the bottom but he refused. 'I am training you to be an entrepreneur, not a manager,' he told me," Leissner recalls.

陈芳曾经很郁闷，为什么法国人做葡萄酒那么轻松，在中国怎么就那么难？她的朋友给了句话，"等过个 200 年，你也容易了。"

是呀！在其他国家已发展了百年的葡萄酒，在中国才刚刚萌芽。这片土地到底适合种什么，怎么种，要靠经验才能知道。现在能做的，就是耐得住寂寞，慢慢来。在她的葡萄园里，有一块很大的试验田，种着目前中国非主流的葡萄品种，像是黑品诺、雷司令、Aglianico（这一品种在中国还没有统一的翻译）。酿出的酒也不对外发售，只作研究。陈芳请我尝了款最新酿造的黑品诺，风格甜美娇羞，期待有一天能公开发售。

陈芳这种慢慢来的想法和中国当下浮躁的大环境显然有些格格不入，这使得她和农民之间的矛盾日益加剧。现在怡园实行的是一半自己种葡萄，一半向农民收购，可是两边的质量差太多。农民的想法非常投机，市场上流行什么，他们就种什么，根本不愿一心一意放在葡萄上面。而且他们求量不求质，即使陈芳已经承诺：如果葡萄达到规定的糖度就给予更高的收购价格。如今，她正努力收回所有的种植权。

Only now has she come to appreciate her father's efforts in schooling her in business. An entrepreneur dares to lose, hence, will take risk, while a manager only makes the decision he or she feels confident with, Leissner observes.

Being young, female and coming from Hong Kong — those characteristics have been a double-edged sword in her career. At the beginning, much older and more experienced staff were her subordinates, and reluctantly so, only at her father's behest. Being young can also mean bold, so she had courage to move forward, she says.

A female vineyard owner is rare, making Leissner and her vineyard more likely to be remembered. Coming from hectic Hong Kong where a can-do attitude prevails, she experienced a collision of culture and values in slow-moving and remote village in north China. Her staff didn't speak English, while her Mandarin was poor.

新一代的传承才刚刚开始，属于陈芳的这段马拉松还远没有结束，一路上，充满着各种诱惑和冲动让她停下来。然而，不跑到最后，没有人知道终点有多绚烂，于是，她坚持奔跑。

路要一步步走，饭要一口口吃，美好的生活还是要继续，不然做葡萄酒也失去了它的意义。陈芳最爱的，就是拉上一大帮朋友在酒庄里吃吃喝喝。前不久，收到她的一封信，说是园里的葡萄熟了，去看看采收，尝尝新酒。另外，酒庄里养了两头猪，一头叫"赤霞猪"，一头叫"品丽猪"，是时候来一场全猪宴了。自家养的猪天然有机，吃起来才香。本来么，美食与美酒就分不了家，本质上都是人们追求味蕾和嗅觉上的愉悦。

每年的秋天是葡萄园最美的时节，亦是酒庄里最忙碌的日子。那一串串翠绿娇小的果实长大了，摆脱原本青春期的稚嫩，开始成熟转色，展现各种风韵，从红得发紫到紫中透着蓝，再到饱满的金黄。

陈芳总会在这个时候，牵着两个女儿的手，赤着脚走在园里，引导她们去享受葡萄酒的美好，从那深浅颜色不一的一杯杯琼浆玉液里感受各种奇妙的香气，有桃子，有蜂蜜。

Life at Goldman Sachs was filled with deadlines and staff commonly worked until midnight, but people in Taigu are accustomed to taking a two-hour afternoon nap and rambling at meetings before getting to the point. Good relations with local government authorities are essential for doing business in China and Grace Vineyard benefits from government support. But dealing with bureaucracy can be difficult.

"You can only adapt yourself to the world and cannot adapt the world to yourself," Leissner observes.

She has grown fond of what she's doing. It helps to have a selective memory that retains the positive, which makes her confident and upbeat.

"Both my personality and team keep me motivated," she says.

Her winemaker sometimes calls her unexpectedly at midnight, telling her "today's wine is amazing."

She is married to an Austrian businessman, and they have two daughters, ages eight and 10.

大女儿 Anatasia 今年 11 岁，在酒庄里最是欢乐，因为最新的单一品种珍藏系列以她来命名。小女儿心里不平衡了，老是和妈妈念叨："为什么姐姐有自己的酒，我就没有？"陈芳已想好要以小女儿来命名即将推出的全新起泡酒了。

"I walk barefoot with my daughters in the vineyard and teach them to appreciate wine, telling them this is a peach note and this is a honey aroma," she says.

A new story of inheritance is just getting started.

What others say

Lu Yang
Wine director at Shangri-La Group

"We are proud and obliged to put Grace Vineyard on our wine lists to convince Chinese customers that China can produce wine as well as other countries and show foreign guests what China can do.

I organized a wine tasting including most of the top Chinese wines such as Silver Heights and Jia Bei Lan and was pleasantly surprised by Judy's wine. Her Chairman Reserve distinguishes itself through its elegant classicness. However, I forecast that the sparkling wines that she is making with traditional method, aging wine on lees for more than four years, will be more surprising."

Phillip Gao
Publisher and editor-in-chief at Le Vin Wine Magazine

"Grace Vineyard respects French winemaking tradition. Wine tastes outstandingly good among domestic wines, especially its finesse and balance. Price performance is also a highlight. The vineyard sees wine as part of agriculture not a kind of industrial production, although production has increased recently. Those industrialized bottles are made to be standardized, satisfying demand for high production and low cost, which is contradictory to the nature of wine."

Li Demei
Lecturer in viticulture at the Beijing University of Agriculture and an award-winning Chinese winemaker

"Five years ago I commented that Grace Vineyard is one of a few well-recognized wineries that are 100 percent made in China, from vine growing and winemaking to marketing. Its Deep Blue is a classical Old World wine made in the New World. I still believe this. Time tells its commitment to quality and consistency. I personally consider that it is so far the best winery in China."

1. 贺兰山酒庄

酒庄成立于1997年前后，位于宁夏贺兰山东麓，银川市西北35公里处的贺兰山滚钟口风景区内，占地面积6000平方米。该区域降雨少，阳光充足，昼夜温差大，为葡萄成熟创造了良好的条件，自古就是中国有名的水果产地。唐朝诗人韦瞻曾作诗《送卢潘尚书之灵武》赞美道："贺兰山下果园成，塞北江南旧有名。"

2. 波龙堡酒庄

酒庄成立于1999年，位于北京市房山区八十亩地村雾岚山脚下，葡萄种植基地占地70公顷。近几年，致力于有机葡萄酒的酿造。

3. 九顶庄园

酒庄成立于2008年，坐落于山东省青岛市来西武备镇的九顶山。葡萄园区占地150公顷，种植赤霞珠、美乐、霞多丽、维欧尼等品种。

4. 天塞酒庄

酒庄成立于2012年11月，位于新疆巴州焉耆县西戈壁，两面环山，地势起伏，为古代丝绸之路西域重镇。酒庄建设面积2万7千平方米，葡萄园占地面积2000亩，目前种植赤霞珠、美乐、品丽珠、设拉子、霞多丽、马瑟兰等品种，多数都酿造成单一葡萄品种葡萄酒。新疆的无沙阳光和少雨气候使葡萄园几乎不受到虫害侵袭，因而不用农药，有机生产。酒庄技术顾问为本书介绍的中国顶级酿酒师李德美。

中国魅力酒庄

中国第一葡萄酒讲师的
讲台和梦想

为梦想而生的人，无论在哪里都散发出一种光芒。在焦点聚集的讲台上，这种光芒是加倍的。可人生有时就是这么残酷，梦想和讲台，你只能选其一。中国第一葡萄酒讲师李晨光选择了前者。

As appealing
as
an emcee

李晨光的英文名是 Steven，翻译成中文是斯帝芬。久而久之，圈内人都习惯称他为斯老师。今年 36 岁的他在过去的五年中，培养了 1600 多名学生，这其中有相当一部分投身了葡萄酒行业，剩下的因为葡萄酒而对生活二字有了新的解读和期待。

第一眼看上去，斯老师并不具备成为一个明星讲师的潜质。像多数中国男人一样，他含蓄，内敛，甚至有些害羞，也缺乏滔滔不绝的好口才。讲台上的他顶着个常年不换，流行于上世纪 80 年代的中分刘海。难怪他曾经的同事，同为葡萄酒讲师的李菲评价道，斯老师是一瓶干邑，不怎么时尚，但够经典。但就是这样一人，一旦他在课堂上抛出个笑点，那种反差所带来的幽默显得特别有张力，"笑果"是加倍的。他曾有个学生对酸味特别不敏感，即便是在品尝 Chablis 的时候，也无法感知其高酸度的特性。斯老师急了："你，你是从山西来的嘛？！"

他擅长用自己那套独特的斯式幽默来解释抽象难懂的葡萄酒理论。在谈及葡萄生长与酒之间的关系时，他慢悠悠地来了句："从这款酒可以看出，其果实的成熟度有问题。糖度够了，但由于生长期太短，味道不够浓郁和集中。就像有些人，年纪到了，但是心理不成熟。"

做斯老师的学生是幸福的，在他的课上，不懂酒体、单宁、橡木桶，喝不出黑醋栗、打火石、皮革味并不会成为太大的负担。于他看来，保护学生的自信心，并引导他们从葡萄酒中获得成就感和快乐远比通过考试，拿到证书要重要得多。为此，他付出了额外的细心和耐心。他大概是中国唯一一个在开课之前详读学生个人资料的葡萄酒讲师。

"要是多数学生都不是业内人士，缺乏一定的葡萄酒基础，我就要调整授课方式和难度，比如把开放式的简答题转变成相对容易的判断题和选择题。不然，他们会有挫败感。而学生来自哪里，从小吃什么长大很大程度上决定了他们对香气的记忆和味道的判断。记忆不同，品酒的逻辑和语言自然也不一样。"斯老师强调。

这样一来，老师自然能理解为什么有些来自上海的学生对葡萄酒中的甜度没有那么敏感，因为他们的妈妈习惯在菜肴里放上几勺糖；来自北方的学生怎么也无法分辨白葡萄酒中番石榴的味道，因为这水果根本不曾在他们的味觉记忆中存在过。

吃到些昂贵的进口水果，算是上他的课能得到的额外福利，比如黑醋栗、蓝莓、覆盆子、车厘子等等。

"这些水果主要生长在西方，于中国人来说并不熟悉，但却是葡萄酒经典品酒词中的一部分。若是你从来没有闻过、尝过，又怎么能在葡萄酒中辨识出他们的味道？"斯老师说道。

Wine educator Li Chenguang is somewhat of a trail blazer in China as he relies on his quick wit, blunt honestly and sense of humor to help his students learn how to appreciate fine wines.

His penchant for cracking jokes during class keeps his students comfortable and relaxed.

"I had one student who just wasn't sensitive to the acidity in wine, even in Chablis (Burgundy white). So, I joked, 'Are you from Shanxi Province (a famous vinegar-producing area)?'"

Aside from his sense of humor, the 35-year-old Shandong Province native boasts strong credentials. He is the first UK-trained Chinese wine educator. He is also one of the few in China with a certificate from the London-based wine school Wine and Spirit Education Trust (WSET), who's qualified to teach level 3. Li, a WSET diploma holder (known as WSET level 4), is only one step away from Master of Wine, the highest title in the industry.

但这些课前准备和教学工具的运用
都不是斯老师最引以为傲的。在他
带领学生拿起酒杯的那一刻，才是
斯老师光芒最闪耀的瞬间，展现出
他和其他老师最大的不同。

在中国，多数葡萄酒讲师都是摇头晃脑地背着 Robert Parker 或是 Jancis Robinson 等酒评家的品酒词，进行所谓的引导式教学：讲师轻晃酒杯，深沉地来一句，明亮的红宝石色，中度酒体，有法国橡木、樱桃草本的味道，收尾绵长。学员接着品酒，感觉仿佛一切都如老师所说的一样。

斯老师却坚持要求学生盲品，并在这个过程中培养出自己独立的品酒思维和词汇。他相信，一旦学生具备了这个能力，那才真正意义上建立了对葡萄酒的自信，并从中获得收益一生的成就感。斯老师的训练呈阶梯式，从对味道和香气最基本的感知开始，像是甜度、酸度、成熟度，再慢慢提升到更细微的感官差异，像是红色水果、黑色水果、热带水果的香气。

"那要是碰到有些学生天生对味觉不敏锐，就是品不出来，连最简单的酸与甜，水果与草本都分辨不出，怎么办？"我问。

"品酒是熟能生巧的，犯错没什么。而且我相信没有教不会的学生，大不了我给他课后辅导，专门找两瓶针对他盲点的酒来训练！"斯老师说得很坚定。

His style and enthusiasm for teaching outside the textbook makes him one of the most respected and influential wine educators in China. He has taught around 1,500 students in the past four years.

Chinese wine educators are mainly based in Shanghai, Beijing and Guangzhou. Since students come from all over the country, the wine courses are often intense — three to five days packed with information and tastings.

Li says this puts a lot of pressure on wine educators.

"I have to stand up in front of the class for eight hours each day," says Li, who's now based in Shanghai.

Li now teaches WSET course; he used to teach ISG (International Sommelier Guide) as well. The WSET courses teach wine theory. The ISG courses are more practical, focusing on things like how to serve wine properly. Each class usually has around 15 students.

A three-day, WSET-2 course costs about 5,000 yuan (US$813) while a five-day, WSET-3 course will set you back about 10,000 yuan.

"离开逸香的那两个月是我人生中最痛苦的日子。一个老师，没了讲台，那真的就什么都没有了。我不知道等待我的未来是什么，心中充满了对未知的恐惧。"回想起来，李晨光有点哽咽。

像斯老师这样一个为讲台而生的人，一旦离开了讲台，是要承受多少彷徨和失落。

2013 年 6 月，一条"金牌讲师李晨光出走逸香"的新闻登上了各大葡萄酒媒体的头条，逸香是中国最大的葡萄酒教育机构，总部位于北京。业界一片哗然，纷纷猜测斯老师的离开背后是否有着不可告人的秘密。

斯老师与逸香之间一直是一种唇齿相依的关系。他成名于逸香，在过去的三年里，他除了是逸香最受欢迎的讲师，还担任培训部经理。逸香也因为斯老师的专业和人气，稳坐中国葡萄酒教育的头把交椅，并逐年扩大经营规模。于逸香来说，斯老师的离开是致命的。他是中国第一批也是逸香唯一一个 WSET diploma 持有者（教授 WSET3 的必备资质）。截至目前，大陆地区拥有这张证书的不到 10 人。这意味着逸香在短期内无法推出 WSET3 课程，自然也就称不上中国第一了。

Li's reputation has grown in the past three years while working for Beijing-based Ease Scent Wine and Culture, widely regarded as the country's biggest wine education provider.

However, wine insiders say Li shocked the industry last July when he resigned at Ease Scent over the company's future direction.

Li quotes a Confucius saying to explain his decision: There's little common ground for understanding people with differing principles.

Ease Scent is transforming itself from an education provider to a center combining wine education, sales, media and IT.

Li admits he clashed with his partner because he refused to alter the wines used for teaching.

"Wine used for teaching is distinctive. It has to be expressive, typically reflecting the character of a wine region and grape, which is often the opposite of market demand," he says.

斯老师对此一直讳莫如深。甚至于，不谈这件事是他接受采访的前提。他只给了一句话："道不同，不相为谋。"

了解斯老师的人都清楚，他把教育当成是一份值得投入一生的事业。而他的前东家似乎是将打造互联网帝国作为其终极梦想，教育只是一块跳板，抑或是一份副业。

"我的偶像是新东方的俞敏洪，他将教育打造成具有商业价值的服务。我的教育梦想就是提供给学生一套完整的服务，从课程注册，课堂教学，课后辅导，考前复习到最终的考试。"斯老师说。

除此之外，教育拥有其他行业所没有的特殊属性，老师的一句话或许会改变学生的一生，教书和育人很难分开，但育人的责任经常和商业利益相冲突。国内有相当一部分葡萄酒教育机构，他们不是明着鼓吹就是含蓄地引导，总之就是让学生相信，只要考出 WSET，就能有份高薪的工作。可斯老师总会在课堂上点穿这个谎言，并向学生揭示一个听上去有些残忍的事实：如果你自己不是那么有钱，如果你指望学葡萄酒来赚钱，那还不如早点离开。因为你根本承受不起那些贵到咋舌的 fine wine（精品酒），而那些所谓的高薪承诺根本就是胡扯。

For example, Sauvignon Blanc from Sancerre, Loire Valley, in east France is unoaked while Chinese wine companies prefer importing oaked wines to suit Chinese customers.

After quitting, Li says he experienced a difficult two months before establishing his own company, Stephen Wine (Stephen is his English name).

"This period was the most miserable part of my life," Li says. "Nothing is holy when an educator loses his podium. I felt lost and I was so confused about my future."

A wine insider who asked not to be named says Li's resignation left Ease Scent's future in doubt.

"For some time after Li left Ease Scent, the training center could not launch any WSET-3 courses since he was the only educator there qualified to teach it," the source says. "Ease Scent may no longer be the industry leader."

Li's teaching idol is Yu Minhong, founder and CEO of New Oriental Education Group, an English language-training center.

没有了学生和讲台，也就没有了成就感和追寻梦想的勇气。斯老师下定决心，要把失去的找回来。几经周折，他于去年在上海自立门户，开班授课，一切重新开始。

"哎！若是为赚钱就不做教育了。"斯老师坦陈，教育的利润空间是微薄的，付出的精力却是巨大的，选择做下去更多地靠梦想来支撑。

中国的 WSET 课程基本上都采取三到五天的密集授课，他在讲台上每天一站就是八个小时。最忙的时候，他一个月开四次课，连轴转。

课堂上品酒用的酒单虽关乎教学质量，却存在着很大的成本压缩空间，多数讲师依赖酒商赞助。甚至可以由此大胆推断，学生们喝到的很大一部分都是积压在仓库里的滞销品。斯老师对独立制定酒单非常坚持，甚至都有些固执了。

"教学用酒承担的功能与商业用酒是完全不一样的。好喝，性价比都不是第一考量，鲜明忠实地反应产区风格才是最重要的。"斯老师强调。

"My philosophy is to create a complete wine experience, from enrolling lesson, classroom teaching, after-class tutoring to attending the final world unified exam," he says.

"Li's professional teaching is complemented by his distinctive sense of humor," says Lu Mengxi, marketing and PR manager of California Wine Institute, who attended one of Li's classes.

Li has a shy, reserved personality and has an old-fashioned haircut parted down the middle.

"When he throws a punch line, it is in sharp contrast with his timid personality and the whole class bursts out laughing," says Li Fei, a wine tutor who once worked for Ease Scent.

Li Chenguang says a good wine educator should be as appealing as an emcee, otherwise students will fall asleep since wine theory can be dull.

He adds that one of his focuses in class is building confidence among students, which leads them to a sense of achievement.

他用法国卢瓦河谷的长相思来举例。在中国卖得好的都是那些经橡木桶熟成的，有着国人喜爱的复杂烘烤香气。但这个产区经典的长相思都不经过陈年，直接饮用，呈现清新的口感。这样的酒，在中国不好卖，因此又贵又难找。

斯老师以他的幽默、耐心、爱心和坚持赢得了学生的尊重和信赖。多数上过他课的学生都成为了他交心的朋友。但这两个月，学生发给他的好多条微信都让他觉得沉重和压抑。有个 WSET diploma 在读的学生写道，学葡萄酒似乎是给自己下了个套，如今陷入了一个动弹不得的泥潭，再也没能力往前迈一步，物质上和精神上都无力承受。

"这样的心情，我都能理解。当年，我也是那样走过来的。"斯老师说着，思绪回到了 10 年前他在英国的那段"光辉岁月"。

Student's profile

"Chinese students have less confidence in wine due to the lack of a wine drinking tradition here," Li says.

He prepares thoroughly, reading every student's profile before class in order to understand everyone's wine base and possible palate.

If most students in a class have little wine knowledge, he will adjust the level of difficulty. For example, he may change open-ended questions on tests to multiple choice and true-or-false questions.

Li believes the area a student grows up in to a large extent influences their palate and ability to identify wine aromas and flavors.

"It's impossible to ask students from northern China to identify guava, a fruit grown in the south, in wine," he says.

He also spends plenty of time sourcing videos and photos to explain abstract and complicated viticulture. For example, he uses a photo of a half-peeled grape to explain the color of wine. He also tries hard to answer questions only Chinese students ask, for example, how to spot a fake wine.

He says fake wines have an obvious artificial flavor and a chemical taste.

他清楚地记得，就是那一瓶具有新世界风格的 Rioja，果香浓郁而奔放。他边喝酒，边看那年的卖座大片《神话》。不知道是因为女主角金喜善太漂亮还是那瓶酒真的好喝，他不知不觉中喝了整整一瓶，打破了自己酒量的历史纪录。

2004 年，斯老师已从山东大学英语专业毕业并做了两年的中学英语老师。此时的他意识到自己并不享受中学老师这种中规中矩的生活，也不清楚自己到底适合做什么。他选择去英国的曼彻斯特，既不为留学也不为工作，就是要看看这个世界到底有多大，也就是西方流行的"gap year"。到那里的第一个周末，斯老师就不淡定了。

他去超市逛逛，顺便买几罐啤酒，却意外地发现在英国，一瓶葡萄酒也就比啤酒贵个 15 元人民币，哪像中国，便宜点的啤酒才 2 块钱，最差的国产葡萄酒却要 48 元。斯老师盘算着，既然没差很多，那不如试试看高大上的吧。一开始，和大多数葡萄酒初学者一样，他只喜欢白葡萄酒，尤其是酸酸甜甜的那一种，像是蓝仙姑 Riesling。斯老师曾经看不懂酒标，挑酒看包装，喝酒用水杯，最经典的故事莫过于把一瓶昂贵的 Sauternes 给扔了，理由是喝上去太甜。他有试着像那些酒评家一样去欣赏波尔多红酒的美，可努力了十多次都以失败告终。

In one class, fresh raspberries and black currants are placed on each student's desk so they can smell and taste them to identify these flavors in wine.

"Most Chinese have never eaten such fruits," says the educator.

Li distinguishes himself from other wine educators by giving his students plenty of blind taste tests rather than just reciting tasting notes.

"This is the best way to develop a student's skill in wine tasting. It also raises their confidence and sense of achievement, which is the key to appreciating wine," he explains. "My class is not about passing an exam but about improving my students' wine experience over the long haul."

He begins by teaching easily identified flavors such as sweetness and ripeness and then asks students to gradually identify subtler and more diverse characters in wine.

"我当时觉得红酒又酸又涩，一点也不好喝，直到 2006 年的那一晚，我遇上了一瓶 Rioja。"斯老师回忆道。

为了能品尝到更多的好酒，斯老师在 2007 年 4 月成为了伦敦私人会所 Morton's Club 的一名侍酒师。这职业很锻炼人，除了能喝到很多名贵的酒，高强度的工作每天要持续到凌晨。他苦中作乐，练就了单手开酒刀，快速开瓶的本领，受用至今。他只要在讲台上露两手，同学们纷纷投以崇拜的目光，瞬间打起精神上课，屡试不爽。同年，他也开始了 WSET diploma 的学习，花了整整三年才拿到证书。

Li says he gives special attention to those with a naturally insensitive nose and palate.

"It doesn't matter if you make a mistake. Practice makes perfect. In the last resort, I can arrange a one-to-one class until you taste right," Li says.

He's warm and caring but also straightforward and tough.

Some of his students take his course because they want to work in the wine industry as a sommelier or sales manager since some education marketers equate a WSET certificate with a high-paid job.

"那段时间很痛苦，甚至于是挫败。我已经品过最少一千种酒，但盲品时，还是一次，又一次，再一次的错！"斯老师回忆道。

如果是在中国，他还能去找朋友倾诉，但他只身伦敦，那种独在异乡为异客的寂寞让斯老师的学习之路更为心酸。他没有放弃过，白天，穿梭于各大品酒会练习盲品。到了晚上，伦敦城里总有一扇窗户亮着灯到深夜，那是斯老师在苦读，房间里放着Beyond乐队的歌，他觉得他们的歌词和旋律传递着励志的正能量。他最爱那首《海阔天空》，里面唱道"多少次迎着冷眼与嘲笑，从没放弃过心中的理想"。

李晨光不是没可能成为中国第一个Master of Wine（葡萄酒大师），这是葡萄酒世界最高的学历之一，也是业内人士的终极梦想。可他对此一点也不乐观，说道："如果通向Master of Wine的路是深渊，那么我就是在搭梯子。甚至，走不到尽头也没关系，我只要能看到它就行了。"

"I reveal the truth about the wine industry: If you are not wealthy enough or have high expectation of making money from wine, don't get involved. Fine wines are expensive and such marketing slogans are just bull poop," Li says.

Walking into a trap

During the recent two months, many of his students, especially those learning WSET-4 — the highest level — confided how difficult it is.

One student says learning about wine is like walking into a trap. It's too difficult to pass and go forward. And he cannot afford the time in order to pass the course or the money for the best wines.

Li empathizes with such students as it brings back memories of his start in the wine world in the UK.

In 2004, after graduating from Shandong University majoring in English and working as a middle school English teacher for two years, Li says he moved to Manchester to begin a new life.

要通过这场号称世界上最难的考试，障碍重重。它对知识的广度有很高的要求，尤其是对全球各产区和消费市场的熟知，这都需要做实地考察。但老师的身份，定期的开课都限制了他时间和行动上的自由。除此之外，绝大多数的市场分析报告、产区介绍都是用法语和英语写的，中国人占尽语言的劣势。

斯老师在考生和老师两个角色中忙碌地穿梭着，刚开完课，就飞到波尔多、香港去读大师班。

采访的时候，我问过斯老师一个问题："如果要选择一款酒来形容你自己，你会选什么？"

他是一拖再拖，一直没给出个答案。

但斯老师最近写的一句微信签名好像说明了些什么：

"我是一瓶老年份的酒，不到开瓶的那一刻，你永远都不知道岁月沉淀带给他的是绝代的风华还是无情的摧残。"

其实斯老师这瓶酒开与不开还有那么重要吗？人如其名，李晨光，用一束晨光温暖了一批又一批的学生，而这些学生正是中国葡萄酒的未来。

On his first weekend in the UK, Li remembers shopping for beer and finding that a bottle of wine cost only 45 yuan, just 15 yuan more than a can of beer. Surprised by how cheap the wine was, he says he decided to try it.

This single decision created a passion for wine.

Li says he loved sweet white wines for a long time, tasting about 10 Bordeaux reds and not being impressed.

"Red wine for me was not tasty, it was sour and bitter until I tried a bottle of Rioja from Spain," he recalls.

One night in 2006, he opened a Rioja at home and drank it while watching the film "The Myth (2005)" starring Jackie Chan.

"That red wine is in the New World style, fruity," he recalls. "The film was so good that I kept drinking without thinking about it. It was the first time I drank a whole bottle on my own."

In 2007, Li became a sommelier at Morton's Club in London in part because he wanted to have access to better wines.

"Being a sommelier has helped me be a better teacher," he says. "When I demonstrate such skills, my students admire and trust me more. My food and wine pairing is also much more professional."

Starting from 2008, he spent two years getting his WSET diploma.

"That was difficult," Li says. "I had tasted thousands of wines but still couldn't do well in blind taste tests."

He persisted though, recalling how he listened to motivational songs like "Boundless Oceans, Vast Skies" by Hong Kong rock band Beyond and filling up his days with studying and numerous tastings.

Li is now working on becoming a Master of Wine although he admits it is his greatest challenge.

"If my way to a Master of Wine is an unfathomable abyss, I am slowly building up my ladder," he says.

"It doesn't matter if I don't reach the final destination as long as I can see it in the distance," he adds.

Q & A

Q: What's your most embarrassing moment in class?

A: When my students taste a wine that I think is enjoyable and they say "undrinkable."

Q: What is the most impressive class you've taught?

A: One time I knew there was a wine columnist attending my class. I prepared well to avoid making any mistake. Finally, he says "you are different than others."

Q: Where does your sense of achievement come from?

A: Definitely blind tasting. I love being able to name the vintage and chateau of a bottle.

Q: What's your favorite wine?

A: Chateau Mouton 2004, elegant and balanced, enjoyable.

1. 赵凤仪

中英混血，剑桥毕业的赵凤仪说得一口流利的中文。如果当她是中国人，那么赵凤仪即将成为中国首位葡萄酒大师。她在北京成立了龙凤美酒顾问公司，致力于 WSET 葡萄酒教育。

2. 唐丽燕

唐丽燕为 ASC 精品酒业大中华区培训经理，WSET Diploma 持有者，曾在美国担任过侍酒师。

3. 徐伟

徐伟，也买酒首席葡萄酒顾问兼培训质检总监，WSET 授权讲师。葡萄酒爱好者更喜欢称他为"小皮老师"。小皮身上有一份与生俱来的幽默感，这让他的课堂总是轻松愉悦。他被誉为葡萄酒行业内最会说相声的奇才。

4. 李华

李华，西北农林科技大学副校长，博士生导师，算得上在中国开展葡萄酒学术教育的第一人。他在西北农林创立了中国第一个葡萄酒学院，培养了一大批包括酒制网创始人侯明，保乐力加资深培训经理郭明浩在内的中国葡萄酒产业中坚力量。

5. 郭明浩

保乐力加资深培训经理，因为学识渊博而被葡萄酒业内人士称为郭校长。这位校长虽然没有任何培训资质，但却在中国普通百姓中颇具影响力。他主持的中国首档葡萄酒脱口秀栏目《漫谈葡萄酒》以葡萄酒为线索，串联了历史上的逸闻趣事，在爱奇艺之平台上获得了很高的点击率，算是普及葡萄酒文化的佼佼者。

中国最具人气葡萄酒讲师

99/119

成也女王，
败也女王

Jancis Robinson 的成就和光芒是个奇迹。今年 65 岁的 Jancis 是全球最多产的葡萄酒作家，先后至少出版了 25 本著作，其中的 2 本《世界葡萄酒地图》、《牛津葡萄酒大词典》更是销量突破 400 万册，被翻译成 14 种语言，被业内人士奉为圣经。她是以行业外身份考取葡萄酒大师的世界第一人，开创了用电视节目普及葡萄酒文化的先河。

Wine rule:
Most pleasure
at lowest
price

一代女王 Jancis Robinson，还是老了。如同她笔下的葡萄酒，再经得起岁月更迭也总有走向衰败的一天。

2014 年的春天，Jancis 来上海为自己的中译本签名售书。女王进入房间的一刹那，能感受到她身上传递出一种强大的能量和气场。她的穿着打扮和年龄并不协调。白色的荷叶边衬衫外面套着一件藏青色的背带裙，顶着一头活泼的齐刘海短发，涂着鲜艳的口红。这样的名人，早已习惯在记者面前端出近乎完美的谦和和礼貌，但眼神里却藏不住傲气和不服老的倔强。

坐在她对面的我心里七上八下，琢磨着该怎样挤出那个让她尴尬的问题。Jancis 刚刚完成了她在上海的评审工作，从 53 款国产葡萄酒中选出 7 款最具国际竞争力的作品，然而结果却饱受争议。

"她的品鉴太违背常理，那些业内口碑良好的酒一个都没评上。很多酒庄对她的品位都是敢怒不敢言，谁让她是 Jancis Robinson 呢？"一位不具名的业内人士感叹。

她已不是第一次受非议。不久前她和中国顶尖的葡萄酒专家们一起访问宁夏葡萄酒产区。当时有一款酒，在场几乎所有的人都辨别出这瓶酒已因为橡木塞污染而坏掉，唯独女王享受地晃杯闻香，慢悠悠地说了句：这是款品质极好的葡萄酒。

"我不否认她是一个伟大的酒评家。但岁月不饶人，感官会随着年龄增长而逐渐老化。"一个长期驻扎在宁夏的葡萄酒专家如是说。

对于 Jancis 来说，这是多么残酷而致命的批判。她的酒评向来以专业、客观、严谨而著称。被她钦点的酒在欧洲的销量会直线上升。要是被她说不好，进这款酒的商家也可以卷铺盖走人了。品酒技能是一个酒评家的生命线。

我终于鼓足了勇气：你觉得年龄增长会影响你品酒吗？

她脸上的表情产生了细微而复杂的变化，给出的回答，有些矛盾。

"不会！相反地，年龄上去，心更静了，我品酒时也更为专注了。嗯，大环境变了，现在消费者们越来越懂酒且自信，酒评家的观点已经不那么重要了。或许等我死后，这个世界已经不需要第三方酒评了，但目前，我还有点用处。"她说道。

WINE critic Jancis Robinson, arguably the most powerful woman in the world of wine, compares herself to a glass of Burgundy — subtle and complex, offering varied sensations.

Burgundy red is known for its aging potential. But Robinson's tasting skill has been called into question by some experts (though not in public, of course) during her recent visit to China. They suggest age has affected tasting acumen.

Asked earlier by Shanghai Daily whether getting older affected her tasting, Robinson replied that her skill is unimpaired and, if anything, age has improved her ability to concentrate.

The 64-year-old British expert was the first person outside the wine trade entitled to write MW (Master of Wine, the ultimate title) after her name.

在牛津男友的引领下，她对葡萄酒局限于欣赏，或者说娱乐。真正严肃地对待它，并用文字记录下来还得从一次窥探之旅说起。

Jancis 这辈子，活脱脱就是一部英国乡村女孩成功登顶上流社会的励志传奇。若是非得从遗传基因里挖出点和葡萄酒相关的，那要追溯到她太外公 James Forfar Dott。老人在法国郊外拥有一片树林，据说是用来从事橡木桶生意。

但到了她这一代，家族已不富有，不可能和精英阶层专属的红色饮料产生丁点交集。

Jancis 出生在英格兰西北部的 Cumbria 郡，位置偏远，快到了和苏格兰交界的地方。这地方整个一大乡村，没有多少现代化的特征，也没有什么历史遗迹，让人印象深刻的是成片的湖泊，延绵的丘陵，还有茂密的森林。

不知是不是急于走出这个小地方，Jancis 从小就很勤奋，一路过关斩将考入了牛津大学的数学专业。她在回忆录里曾经写道：在我的那所中学，平均一年仅一个毕业生能考入牛津或是剑桥。

The prolific writer has published at least 25 books, including two that are considered wine bibles, "The World Atlas of Wine" and "The Oxford Companion to Wine." She produces the world's first TV series on wine aired by the BBC.

As the whole world becomes more knowledgeable about wine, consumers feel more confident of their own opinions, and wine critics are needed less and less.

"All ordinary wine drinkers will become experts after I'm dead. So I still get a few years to be helpful," Robinson tells Shanghai Daily.

She was in town to sign the Chinese edition of "Jancis Robinson's Wine Course," organized by ASC Fine Wines, and to conduct a 2-day tasting together with two other critics, Bernard Burtschy and Ian D'Agata.

They chose the seven most competitive bottles among 53 Chinese wines at the Chinese Wine Summit.

爱情是极容易滋生于这座浪漫而古老的大学里的。成天穿梭于那些中世纪古典建筑，处处是罗马廊柱，哥特尖顶和巴洛克浮雕。每栋教学楼前几乎都有大小不一的花园，种着果树，开着鲜花。在那里，Jancis 遇到了男友 David。这位绅士手拿钥匙，开启了 Jancis 通向葡萄酒的大门。

David 出身书香门第，对于吃喝颇有造诣，这也成了两人约会的重点。Jancis 清楚地记得在牛津郊外一家叫 Rose Revived 的餐厅，David 为她打开了一瓶 Chambolle Musigny, Les Amoureuses 1959。那瓶酒对她来说影响深远。这是瓶产自勃艮第的红酒，并不像波尔多那些结构庞大的葡萄酒那般晦涩难懂。

"每一口都让我着迷，一种难以用文字所形容的美。我不确定当时两个人到底有没有讨论这款酒还是光顾着闷头享受了。" Jancis 回忆道。

David 的父亲是个来自德国的教授。每每到男朋友家去玩，都会看到他父亲保留着德意志上流社会的生活习惯。晚餐一定要有啤酒，结束之后，打开留声机，让舒伯特或是莫扎特的旋律缓缓地流出。当整间屋子沉静下来，他打开最爱的 Mosel 雷司令。

"She's still powerful enough to influence a wine's market performance. But that doesn't mean I will change my wine style to please her," says Deng Zhongxiang, a French-trained Chinese winemaker at Ningxia Lilan Winery.

Some wineries do change their styles to please Robinson or powerful critic Robert Parker, who both give scores to wines.

'Nowhere near great'

Robinson says the best Chinese wine she tasted on this trip is Kanaan Winery Cabernet Sauvignon 2011, which she called "very honest and interesting, well balanced." Noting that the wine is made by a woman (Wang Fang), she says,

"Three Chinese winemakers that I remember, whose wines impress me, are all women."

However, Robinson has reservations about the quality and diversity of Chinese wine in general.

"I still think Chinese wine is nowhere near great wine, but I do understand there's a will to make (great wine)," she says.

直到现在，Mosel 雷司令仍是 Jancis 自家酒窖里最特别的收藏，其中让她最骄傲的是瓶 1971 年份的 J.J. Prum Wehlener Sonnenuhr Auslese。

"记得我在 1988 年的新年夜开了一瓶。酒的颜色已泛出金黄，但边缘仍透出一丝青绿。这酒还是充满活力，只不过多了点陈年的香气和矿物感，甚至微微有些香料的气息。它在口中轻快地舞动，可味道深处藏着扎实和深邃。"Jancis 将对这瓶酒的体会写入了自己的回忆录。

牛津大学的各大学院地下藏着全欧洲最让人艳羡的酒窖，自 19 世纪前后藏酒至今，有许多快绝迹的稀世珍品。大学的教职员工拥有以较低价格买酒的特权。其中 All Souls 学院的酒窖颇为神秘。它只对在学校举足轻重的学术权威们开放，一般在校生是进不去的。Jancis 对此充满好奇，几经周折，她说服了当时掌管酒窖钥匙的 Walter Quelch。建于 17 世纪末的酒窖庞大而昏暗，这是她第一次见到成箱成箱的 1961 年份波尔多一级庄。

Chinese wine also does not yet have a track record of improving with time, she adds.

Robinson says it's "amazing" that China, as the world's fifth (in volume) wine producer, still produces an extremely narrow range, dominated by Cabernet and Merlot reds and Chardonnay whites.

"How are you ever going to move on unless you expose consumers something else?" she says.

Robinson attributes this in large part to history and the popularity of "flying winemakers" or foreign experts for hire.

Initially, when China was falling in love with wine, Bordeaux (mainly made with Cabernet grapes) was driving the market, she says.

Flying winemakers (predominantly French and Australian) have helped China's wine industry but they have also heavily influenced the expression of local characteristics, she says.

"The best wines express a place, a person, and a point in the historical continuum," Robinson writes in her book "Tasting Pleasure: Confessions of a Wine Lover."

这世上有人为了钱而工作，有人为了爱。Jancis 属于后者。

大学毕业后，Jancis 并没有如愿从事葡萄酒行业而是在旅行社里待了一年。但这段经历倒是为她日后高效率奔走于全球各大酒庄提供了些许帮助。直到 1975 年 12 月 1 日，她终于以助理编辑的身份昂首走进了一栋位于伦敦 soho 区，毗邻摄政街的大楼，那是葡萄酒与烈酒杂志的办公地。那年她 25 岁。

"葡萄藤总是长在这世上最美的那些角落。地中海气候，除了孕育出葡萄也是打造旅游胜地的必要条件。"她回忆道。

除了造访产区，葡萄酒编辑的另一工作重心就是参加一场接一场的品酒会。对于人生的第一场正式品酒会她仍记忆犹新，且充满感恩。

那天，列席参加的都是业内资深人士，包括 Hugh Johnson，全球最具影响力的葡萄酒作家。年轻的 Jancis 谨小慎微，也不敢说出自己到底喝到了什么，生怕被贻笑大方。让她更为惊叹的是，同一款酒，每个人说出来的答案天差地别。

"这酒有点酸涩，不是吗？"

She calls the flaws in Chinese wine "stylistic rather than technical."

The quality of some oak for aging barrels is not very good, some reds are too sweet, unbalanced and "lack fruit weight on the mid palate," she observes.

Mislabeled wines

Cabernet Gernischt, a local variety, doesn't ripen properly, bringing out wine's natural green acidic characteristics, she says, adding that winemakers may compensate for that by leaving a lot of sugar in the wine.

"The biggest challenge is to ensure that all wines are authentic," she says, referring to the problem of fakes and mislabeled wines. "There should be a definite correlation between what is said on the label and what is in the bottle ... to ensure all the wines are 100 percent made from grapes."

"这酒有着漂亮的圆润感。"

"这酒的酸度还应该加强些。"

有意思的是，大家谁也不反驳别人，可谁都坚持自己的。

Jancis 意识到，品酒是种非常主观的体验。要是碰到好的前辈，他们会鼓励你自信地说出自己的感受。她还记得当时自己零星地蹦出了几个词，现在想想，应是被人看来古怪而幼稚的，但当时没有一个人面露疑惑或不屑。

She expressed concern that many Chinese get the wrong impression of wine because of a first tasting experience with a bad domestic wine or a cheap, imported bottle.

Robinson says she is impressed by the quality wines, citing her visits since 2002 to Shanxi Province, Beijing, the Xinjiang Uygur and Ningxia Hui autonomous regions.

In Ningxia the local government is trying to develop the wine industry, she notes in the seventh edition of "The World Atlas of Wine," devoting a section to the area.

On this China trip, Robinson visited Yunnan Province to see a new wine project invested by the LVMH Group.

随着 Jancis 越来越资深，她参加的评酒会的级别也是水涨船高。她是全世界为数不多品尝过那批神秘天价葡萄酒的人。上世纪 80 年代末，德国收藏家 Hardy Rodenstock 声称他在巴黎一个尘封废弃的老酒窖里发现了一批印有美国总统托马斯·杰弗逊签名的波尔多名庄。其中一瓶 1787 年的拉菲更是在 1985 年由佳士得拍出了 105000 英镑的天价。但这批酒的真假一直是个世纪悬案。

Jancis 喝的是其中一批 1787 年份的木桐庄。当时，所有的人都凝神屏气地等待着这瓶陈放了近 200 年的老酒的表现。香气一开始很封闭，但渐渐地，一层厚厚的甜美包裹了整个房间。

"时任佳士得名酒部总监的 Michael 说味道像是浸泡过的姜饼，Hardy 想到了甜美的咖啡，但我觉得是那种高级润滑油的味道。说实话我不喜欢，但确实是瓶好酒。" Jancis 写在她的回忆录里。

把那些抽象的品酒记忆变成具象的文字或许是存在于葡萄酒写手（到了 Jancis 这级别应该称呼为作家）和侍酒师之间最大的不同。而 Jancis 的女性身份赋予了其文字独有的细腻与敏锐。

In her latest tasting of Chinese wines, Robinson's judgement was questioned by some Chinese wine experts and writers, since many acclaimed labels didn't make it through to the finals.

"Her tasting judgment is contrary to our general expectation. Many wineries are unconvinced but dare not say so because she is Jancis Robinson," says one wine insider, asking that his name not be published.

Her tasting, actually, has been questioned in the past. According to another insider, Robinson and leading Chinese wine experts visited Ningxia not long ago and were served a bottle that everyone else thought was corked except for Robinson, who insisted that it was a very good wine.

"I believe she is a great taster, but she's not that young. Her nose and palate may have begun to degenerate," says the insider, asking not to be identified.

Wine tasting is a lifelong pursuit for critics, so doubts can be devastating. Asked about skeptics, Robinson says with a laugh, "I definitely haven't got older (as a taster).

比如，她在写加州之旅时描述道：
"我总是把这地方和特殊的气味联系在一起。那是种温暖而甜蜜的气息，混合着树脂还有阳光照耀在红杉木上的味道，还有那无处不在的肉桂味儿。"

她是这样写加拿大冰酒的甜美和酸度："这感觉就像是游走于最纯美的葡萄汁和脸上被猛地扇了一记耳光之间。"

她犀利的观点时常带有批判性，这使得其在英国金融时报上的专栏长盛不衰。有意思的是，她的爆发力永远是藏在笔下，和她面对面时是断然觉察不到的。

"作为一个（酒庄）访问者，我会客客气气，但一旦写成文字，我非常冷静客观，甚至可以说是到了冷酷的地步。我从来不会去考虑写下这些东西可能造成的后果。"她写道。

"But I find that as I get older, my ability to concentrate becomes much better," she adds.

Women have a physiological advantage in tasting, Robinson says. When scientists measure tasting ability, from consistency to the ability to spot characteristics, experienced women tasters do better than men, she says.

Western societies don't expect women to know much about wine when it's ordered in restaurants.

"Instead of worrying about choosing the right wine, we just choose the wine we feel like drinking," she emphasizes.

"On the macro level, when people are making a seating plan, I will often be put next to the most important person," she says.

Whatever critics say, Robinson is one of the most experienced wine tasters.

"Some of the best wines I've ever had have been old Bordeaux but there is so much else. My most impressive memory is a 1947 Cheval Blanc, a very famous Saint Emilion," she says.

"我的酒窖里是不会放中国酒的。就目前看，没有线索表明中国葡萄酒有陈年的能力。中国本地品种蛇龙珠酿出的酒，喝起来既青涩又不平衡，估计是葡萄没有很好地成熟。"她说道。"很难想象这个国家虽已是全球第五大葡萄酒生产国，但品类却是如此单一，红葡萄酒基本上就赤霞珠和美乐，白的几乎都做成霞多丽。这局限了中国消费者的视野，也势必让这个产业停滞不前。"她在采访中说道。

在有限的品类里，酒的口味也缺乏个性和辨识度。在她看来，最好的酒应该是与众不同的，能表现一片风土、一个时代和一种情怀。可惜的是在中国，占据主导地位的却是那些来自法国和澳洲的飞行酿酒师（长期飞赴全球各产区进行技术指导的酿酒师）。他们酿造的到底是法国酒、澳洲酒，还是全球化环境下的畸形产物？答案有待商榷。但有一点可以肯定，瓶子里没多少中国味。

"于中国来说，还有一件棘手的问题就是假酒。标签上说的和瓶子里装的是不是一回事？而这所谓的葡萄酒是不是真的由葡萄酿造？"Jancis 说到这里，眼角露出一丝不屑。

她虽未挑明，但很明显，在影射中国的假拉菲和掺水葡萄酒。Jancis 倒不是没来由地妄下论断，她跑过的中国产区比很多中国人还要多。从 2012 年至今，她先后走访了山西、北京、宁夏、新疆四大产区。就在接受完采访的第二天，她又马不停蹄地飞到云南去考察由 LVMH 投资的新葡萄酒项目。

颇为讽刺，身为一个中国记者，笔者很多关于中国葡萄酒产业的丑闻却是通过 Jancis 一篇篇专栏揭露获知的。

Jancis 的葡萄酒哲学：让更多人能以最低的成本获取最大的快乐。牛津数学系毕业的她把老师的一句话当成座右铭：数学家就是为了各种节省而存在的。笔耕不辍，让她在短时间内获得了葡萄酒业内高度的认同和尊敬。然而，真正让她为大众所熟知的是 Jancis 于上世纪 70 年代末开创的那本 Drinker's Digest，简称 DD。这是英国第一本站在消费者角度，围绕性价比撰写的葡萄酒手册。一经推出获得了广泛的回响，成为了很多消费者购买葡萄酒时参考的价格标尺。

Jancis 写得有多接地气？

"我们告诉你哪里能买到 6 英镑的酩悦香槟！ 1969 年份的唐培里侬香槟王花 14 英镑就能搞定！"诸如此类。

她认为 DD 的推出很大程度上顺应了英国国情："美国人愿不计一切代价买到最好的，但英国人不同，在吃喝方面，不能花一分冤枉钱。"

她的努力或多或少起些作用。1980 年代初期，英国葡萄酒市场开始了一段从精英垄断走向大众消费的转型。转型期间，总有很多矛盾的画面以及畸形的消费心态，和当下的中国颇有几分相像。

Jancis 似乎是嗅到了全民追捧葡萄酒的感觉，不论男女。就连出租车上的司机也时不时地向她说教葡萄酒的饮用："要是我和女朋友两个人晚上喝，两瓶就够了。"

但另一方面，人们接触葡萄酒的初衷不是因为味道，而是炫耀品位。似乎喝了葡萄酒就晋升到了另一个阶层。她觉得大众对葡萄酒缺乏正确的认识。在这样的环境下，她有了更大的动作。

Jancis 走上了电视荧屏，随着她主持并参与制作的葡萄酒节目在 BBC 的热播，葡萄酒文化开始真正意义上在英国乃至整个西方英语国家得到了普及。

开始，写惯报纸杂志专栏的她低估了电视镜头呈现葡萄酒的难度。一年里的绝大部分时间，酒庄和葡萄园如水一般沉静，偶尔一阵风吹来，葡萄藤上的叶子应付地扭扭腰。对于定格画面的摄影师来说，这是天堂，但对于讲求画面动感和节奏的电视摄像来说，无疑是个大问题。想象一下，几十秒镜头里的画面一动不动，是多么的无聊。

Jancis 无奈之下尽可能把拍摄集中在 9 到 10 月份，酒庄的收获季，也是工人们最忙最不愿意被拍摄的时候。也不知道事前的沟通和协调经历了多少困难，但最终呈现的电视画面是美丽而精彩的：

在葡萄园连绵起伏的波尔多，玛歌庄的工人们大清早就拿起剪刀背着竹篮开始采收葡萄了。采收的前几天，刚下了场雨，葡萄园有些泥泞。人们在泥地上走着，溅起的泥浆就像是画家手中的颜料落在了靴子上、裤管上，形成不怎么难看的像礼花般的渍迹。酒庄的除梗机、压榨机开启，发出哐当哐当的声音，深红透着紫韵的葡萄汁慢慢地流淌出来，在阳光下格外闪亮。在木桐庄庄主罗斯柴尔德男爵（现已去世）的卧室里，老先生穿着他的丝绸睡衣，讲述着其在加州的最新项目——作品一号。

She has also tasted fakes. Robinson is one of the few people who tasted the Thomas Jefferson Bottles, the rarest and most controversial wines that broke auction records but were finally determined to be fake.

"I was extraordinarily lucky to be there (Jefferson's Mouton Tasting), the only journalist ... among the 19 tasters," she says in her book, "Tasting Pleasure."

"The pre-revolutionary bouquet was reticent at first and then built up to a great cloud of sweetness hanging over the whole room," she says.

Robinson decided to go for the Master of Wine title while she was working on a BBC TV series in 1994. At that time, a journalist compared her to a glass of Beaujolais, "flighty and evanescent."

Her reaction, "I will show you that I am not!" Robinson recalls. She adds that her pregnancy at that time helped her excel in tasting.

Her practical, down-to-earth philosophy has contributed to her popularity.

"It (wine) should provide as much pleasure for as many people at the lowest possible cost," she says.

在法国拍摄的时候，Jancis 的女儿 Julia 刚出生没几天。整个拍摄可以说是在喂奶、哄孩子和导演说"1,2,3, 开始"间交替进行的。

专题片一经播出，反响热烈。Jancis 和 BBC 乘胜追击，推出又一档以葡萄品种为主题的系列片，将拍摄范围扩大到全世界，意图将葡萄酒的旧世界和新世界完整地呈现在观众面前。这次的拍摄同样开阔了 Jancis 的视野，各地不同的文化和思维方式一次又一次地突破着这位英国女士的局限。

为了拍摄德国莫塞尔产区的全景，包括起伏的山谷，蜿蜒的河流，河两旁陡峭的斜坡，古老的钟楼，Jancis 第一次亲历了如此丰富的交通方式：热气球、火车、马、摩托车、皮划艇、骡子。

在西班牙北部的 Ribera del Duero，Jancis 惊叹于当地仍保留了质朴而原始的乡村生活方式。马仍是最主要的交通工具。那里的老爷爷会推着独轮手推车回家吃午饭，里面装着一大坛酒。

在意大利西北部的皮尔蒙特，当地人的好客，分享食物之大方已到了夸张的程度。

"如果我们不叫停，他们的菜会一道接着一道上！"Jancis 在回忆录中写道。

在澳洲的阿德莱德，民众的友善和当地的阳光一样的温暖。一个司机把车停在了酒店马路对面，一路帮 Jancis 背着重重的行李，穿过车水马龙的大街，护送她到了酒店。

就在她拍摄电视节目如火如荼的同时，Jancis 还完成了一项于当对 Jancis 来说，参加漫长而艰辛的葡萄酒大师考试，就像是登顶珠穆朗玛峰，成功的那一刻，如释重负，又交杂着成就感和兴奋。

时看来近乎不可能的任务，以全世界第一个非葡萄酒行业人士的身份通过了 Master of Wine（葡萄酒大师）的考试，这之间还穿插着和丈夫 Nick 孕育新的小生命。

参加考试的初衷源于她不服输的个性。上电视虽让她出了名，也招来了些略显刻薄的声音。如果说 Jancis 当时的正面形象是个充满朝气，将精英文化引入普通民众的使者，那么与之相对应的负面形象则是持有哗众取宠的高调，没多少真材实料却穿梭于各大酒庄的花蝴蝶。当时一个葡萄酒作家曾公开发表文章将她比作是一支轻佻的、转瞬即逝的薄若来（该酒以经不起陈年著称），背后的用意不言而喻。

"那篇文章让我最终下定决心在 1984 年参加葡萄酒大师的考试。"Jancis 在回忆录中写道。

高强度高难度的盲品是导致这考试低通过率的一大原因。因此，

Jancis 和同期考生组成学习小组进行练习，频次不断增加，到考前一周已是每日一练。为了不影响各自的工作，模拟练习都放在每天清晨。

"我是到那时才意识到原来薄荷牙膏会影响品酒的准确。"她回忆道。

随着大考时间临近，小组成员中有人是紧张中夹杂着期待和自信，有人透着恐慌和无助。终于，那一天到来了。Jancis 清楚地记得是个周二的早晨，考生们都像是运动员一般蓄势待发。怀有 5 个月身孕的 Jancis 挺着大肚子走进了那间放满酒杯的房间。

"怀孕中的我根本不想喝酒，这倒让我在整场考试中保持着头脑的清

醒和兴奋。不像有些人在盲品过程中会在吐酒之前不小心咽下几口，而酒精无疑会让人昏沉。"Jancis 回忆着。

在 Jancis 的盲品过程中，最精彩却又无法解释的就是直觉。把鼻子探进杯子，就那么轻轻一闻，她不假思索地给出答案。

"有些时候，你就是知道，就是知道那是杯来自法国的设拉子。"她写道。

考完试，她和丈夫去海边小镇 Cornwall 度假。那天早上，夫妻俩正在露台上就着海浪的声音吃着早餐，一个邮差按响了门铃。Jancis 心头一阵紧张，成绩出来了。

门打开，邮差把一个棕黄色的大信封交到 Jancis 手上。她瞬间舒了口气，如果是坏消息，那只是寥寥数语，会装在个小信封里。把信封慢慢撕开的那种过瘾的感觉，她至今仍能回忆得清清楚楚。信封里除了一封简短的祝贺信，还有串很长很长，作为葡萄酒大师必须遵守的条文，其中有一条，永远不卖假酒。如今的 Jancis 已不再是当年那个略带自卑的乡村女孩。她被英女王授予了大不列颠帝国勋章，以表彰其在餐饮领域作出的贡献。虽然刚刚从 WSET（英国葡萄酒与烈酒教育基金会）名誉主席的位子上退下来，但其葡萄酒学术权威的地位仍难以撼动。

她努力且成功地在英国这个略保守且等级森严的国度实现了"只要有梦想，一切皆有可能"。

但那些曾经喜欢她的人却觉得距离她越来越遥远。

一个中国葡萄酒爱好者在文章中写道："你去看 Jancis Robinson

那两部葡萄酒砖头书，讲到雪利酒，其中一句话让我足感羡慕嫉妒恨，她说'本书作者'都'只喝'直接从桶中取出来的，未经过滤的那种，专业术语叫 En Rama。她要告诉大家，老百姓喝不到。"

作者的措辞或许偏激了些，但或多或少能感受到今日的 Jancis 有那么些脱离大众的味道。回顾她的过去，正是拉近了葡萄酒与大众的距离，令她获得了成功。

不禁想起泰戈尔那首《鱼和飞鸟》的诗：

世界上最遥远的距离
不是树与树的距离
而是同根生长的树枝
却无法在风中相依

世界上最遥远的距离
不是星星之间的轨迹
而是纵然轨迹交汇
却在转瞬间无处寻觅。

但愿我们是多虑了，或许 Jancis，仍然是那个 Jancis。

Robinson, a self-described girl from a village school, went on to study math and philosophy at St Anne's College, Oxford.

She fell in love with wine when a boyfriend ordered a bottle of Chambolle-Musigny Les Amoureuses 1959 at Rose Revived restaurant outside Oxford.

She says she enjoys "nothing more than to idle in every wine shop" to enrich her wine cellar.

"I only buy wines which I think worth aging. My cellar is quite conventional. There are quite a lot of Bordeaux, Burgundy, Rhone and a lot of German Riesling, which lasts a very long time, though not everybody realizes it," she says.

1.James Suckling

美国人，在全球最具影响力的葡萄酒杂志 Wine Spectator 担任编辑近 30 年，并于 2010 年成立了自己的葡萄酒网站，发布自己的酒评以及飞往世界各大酒庄的采访实录。

2.James Halliday

Halliday 来自澳洲，被誉为全球范围内点点评澳洲葡萄酒的权威。他也是名成功的葡萄酒作家，先后出版了 40 多本著作。

3.Michel Bettane

Bettane 是法国最有影响力的葡萄酒评家和葡萄酒作家，为法国权威葡萄酒杂志 La Revue du vin de France 供稿长达 20 年。他也是欧洲第一个判断 1982 年为波尔多跨时代意义年份的酒评人。

4.Jose Penin

Penin 于 1980 年创立了西班牙第一份葡萄酒杂志 Bouquet。之后，他长期担任自由撰稿人，逐渐在酒评界崭露头角。1990 年，他出版了《Guia Penin de los vinos de Espana》，一本关于西班牙葡萄酒的指南，就此奠定了其在世界范围内点评西班牙酒的权威地位。

5.Steven Spurrier

说到英国人 Spurreir 先生，不得不提到一场关乎于美国和法国的一场没有硝烟的战争。1976 年，他在巴黎举办了一场盲品比赛，汇聚了法国和美国最好的葡萄酒。结果美国加州的葡萄酒出乎意料地在评委当中获得了极高的分数，战胜了法国酒。法国葡萄酒曾经长期一家独大的时代就此终结。葡萄酒历史上，这场盲品也叫"巴黎审判"。

可能是世上
最公正独立的
酒评家

2012 年，Robert Parker 把自己创立的葡萄酒评分报告杂志《葡萄酒倡导者》卖了，并卸任这本杂志的主编。从此，他的打分不再如往日般影响深远，足以改变这个世界。但人们纷纷开始想念由这个"大鼻子"领衔的年代，很多人曾从中大赚一笔，他们或得到商业利润，或提升了生活品质，还有的则因他而建立了自信。

A nose
for
controversy

酒评家 Robert Parker 给自己的鼻子投了一百万美金的保险。他那硕大而昂贵的鼻子拥有强大而精准的记录功能，储存着上百万瓶葡萄酒的不同香气。人们亲切地称呼他"大鼻子"。

我却更喜欢称他为英雄，一个为推翻上流社会长期把持葡萄酒特权，揭竿而起的平民英雄。然而，英雄终究只属于一个时代。深谙此道的 Parker 选择亲手终结自己的时代。

当时舆论一片哗然，有人说他疯了，也有说是缺钱不得已才卖，还有人说这是见好就收的明智之举。这背后到底隐藏着无奈还是释怀，隐退还是新的期待，没人知道。

坊间曾流传着这样一句话："这酒如果被 Parker 打了 95 分，你根本拿不到货；要是 90 分以下，你也找不到货，因为没人敢卖。"连银行都将他的分数视作分析指数，来决定是否贷款给葡萄酒公司。

那个时候的 Parker，全世界为之疯狂。他来上海浦东香格里拉主持一场晚宴，门票价格炒到了 28888 元，最后被疯抢一空。

每年他要发布评分报告之前，全美经销商们都紧张得睡不着觉，到处打听消息："你听清楚他喝了之后说的是 wow（语气词表示惊叹和赞美）还是 whoa（语气词表示有所保留）？"

这关乎他们一夜暴富还是破产。

THE world's most influential wine critic believes China has a lot of potential to produce high-quality vintages.

Robert Parker, the American wine critic who is recognized as bringing a pro-consumer approach to wine reviews, tells Shanghai Daily, "The Chinese wine I served five years ago was good, but not inspirational. But what I tasted yesterday in Hong Kong convinced me that China is a vast country with diverse soils and climates."

在地球的另一端法国，波尔多那些酒庄庄主们喋喋不休地骂着 Parkerization（帕克化，新名词，表述全球葡萄酒厂商致力于酿造迎合帕克的口味）：都是这个没文化的美国佬把整个市场给搞乱了，人人都不做自己的酒了，都去谄媚地迎合他的口味了。边骂着，边寻思着怎样才能做出 Parker 喜欢的那种感觉。

有人把 Parker 评分超过 95 分的酒做了个整理和总结，发现一些共同特征：厚重的口感，浓郁而集中的成熟水果的甜美，有力的丹宁，雄浑饱满的酒体。

大鼻子对此并不买帐，脸瞬间沉了下来："莫名其妙，这根本就是不实指控。我不觉得自己的口味那么明确而固定。要是你仔细看过我所有的酒评就会发现，我的喜好是非常多元的。"

圈内人都知道 Parker 是个随和不怎么情绪化的人。显然，"帕克化"这个词掐中了他的死穴。

"这说法对 Parker 并不公平。在他的高分目录里也有不少酒体细瘦、药草味明显的葡萄酒，像是新西兰的长相思、卢瓦河谷的红酒。"知名作家 Elin McCoy 在她那本关于 Parker 的传记中写道。

Parker, who was in Shanghai last Saturday for a dinner costing 28,888 yuan (US$4,545.81) per person at Pudong Shangri-La Shanghai, is an independent voice and his opinions often differ from established views.

Parker is plain spoken and not afraid to say what he thinks, even if it will offend people in the industry.

Although the Wall Street Journal earlier this month reported that Parker's influence is declining, his status remains strong in China.

Many wealthy Chinese loyally follow his reviews, buying the Bordeaux wines he rates highly.

The buyers are sometimes criticized as a group of wealthy people without knowledge of wine that push up prices of Bordeaux vintages.

Parker disagrees.

直到如今，帕克化虽不再根深蒂固，但残留的印记和影响力仍挥之不去。在加州的一个酒庄里，我和一个当地葡萄酒讲师品尝着他们出品的最新年份。

"那么浓郁的果味，绝对是 Parker 喜欢的风格。"这个胖胖的美国人把头埋进酒杯里，深吸一口气，坚定地说道。

"这世界上还会有第二个 Parker 吗？"我问。

"恩，"他迟疑了下，"不会再有了，他是时代的产物。"

"I think it's a dangerous insult to Chinese," says the 64-year-old. "It's true that wine producers, led primarily by people from Bordeaux, see China as a great dragon that can consume their wine. But many people with wealth are willing to pay for wines because they love it just like what happened 25 years ago, a time when Americans were the biggest buyers of Bordeaux wine."

Parker predicts that Chinese investment in Bordeaux wines will continue for some time but it will become more difficult in the near future. At a recent wine auction in Hong Kong, he saw signs of Bordeaux wines coming down in price, which he thinks is good.

Further, Parker says there is absolutely no reason Chinese can not appreciate wine. He says the country's tea-drinking tradition means Chinese already have an appreciation of tannins.

"The tannins in wine have the same texture impressing in the mouth as those in green and black tea," he says. "For Chinese, it's not a foreign substance but something they already know. For Americans growing up with milk and Coca-Cola, we should cultivate the taste for tannins."

He says the rich tannins in young Bordeaux wines and California Cabernets are similar to those in green tea.

He also says Chinese food goes very well with wine, contrary to mainstream opinion.

和 Parker 同期的其他作者既不喜欢公开自己品酒的样品，也不喜欢将自己的观点以如此坚定的语气陈述出来。一来，要和读者保持距离，二来，也无法承受自己万一判断失误的后果。本书中另一位与 Parker 齐名的酒评家 Jancis Robinson 就在自己的书中写道："也不知道他哪来的那份自信？"

造就了 Parker 的时代始于 70 年代。那时的美国正酝酿着一场巨大的变革。经济发展迅速，白手起家的创业风潮一浪高过一浪，资本的迅速积累让那些出身不富裕的美国中产阶级开始踏入原本被精英和世家垄断的上流社会，并产生提高生活品质的向往。即使你没有一个收藏葡萄酒的老爸，不懂法语，没去过欧洲，也有权享受这种酒精饮料带来的愉悦。

这股新的消费力量使得当时那些主流的葡萄酒刊物和酒评文字显得不合时宜。当时英语世界里的葡萄酒作家几乎都是熟读法语，游历欧洲的英国人，笔下的文字充斥着高高在上的傲慢、闭塞和以自我为中心的精英主义。他们的文字深受欧洲古典主义的影响，抽象而晦涩。比如，很少有人能读明白他们所说的"贵族式的幽雅和精致"是什么味道？又比如为什么他们要说勃艮第的红酒如同是 30 岁的少妇，博若莱的红酒像是娇嫩的少女？

"There's a myth in the Western world that wine does not work with Chinese food," he says. "I found that Cantonese food and Shanghainese cuisine goes fabulously well with all kinds of wine. Even for spicy Sichuan cuisine, I admit that the pairing should be more careful, white wines such as Riesling and Sauvignan Blanc match well."

The wine dinner at Pudong Shangri-La Shanghai featured first growth wines such as Chateau Latour, including the great vintages of 1982 and 2003. Over the years, Parker has been vilified by some in the industry and praised by others.

Elin McCoy, wine columnist for Bloomberg News and author of "The Emperor of Wine," the first biography about Parker, has described him as "the oenological equivalent of Einstein's brain."

与此同时，旅法美食作家 Julia Child 的书在美国持续畅销。她在书中用大量的笔墨描绘法国人对于生活品质的追求，尤其是美食与美酒。精致餐酒的概念随之深入人心，美国人开始审视自己过于简单且不健康的汉堡可乐文化。

紧随其后的是 1976 年那场由英国人 Steven Spurrier 举办的巴黎审判。在这场盲品大赛中，美国加州的葡萄酒历史性地战胜了法国波尔多和勃艮第的名庄，无疑激发了美国人文化上的自信。

在这样的时间点，美国民众需要一个人，和他们一样出身草根，站在他们的立场上，用他们听得懂的语言介绍葡萄酒。他们需要一个值得信赖且强大有力的声音为他们掏出去的每一笔买酒的钱负责任。而与之完美契合的这样一个人物 Parker 正在美国东部的马里兰州悄悄地长大。

从蹒跚学步到基础教育，大鼻子的活动范围几乎都在一个叫 Monkton 的小地方，平淡到只有农场和田野，以那些英国作家的标准看，甚至散发着些土气。街上发的传单上印着永远不会进入 Parker 试饮名单的 Beringer white，一种廉价的用仙粉黛葡萄酿造的甜型葡萄酒。

今日大鼻子那种舍我其谁的霸气在儿时就显露端倪。高中时，Parker 是学校的足球明星。为了踢进球，他几乎是豁出命地奔跑和争抢。男生运动时散发的迷人荷尔蒙让一个叫 Pat 的姑娘在球场边看得如痴如醉。

两人很快爱得火热。在 Pat 18 岁的生日派对上，大鼻子喝了这辈子第一杯真正意义上的葡萄酒。可惜那天他喝了个大醉，留下的回忆也是痛苦的。他只记得自己趴在马桶上大吐一通，一旁的空酒瓶贴着 Gallo 的酒标。

两年后，Pat 作为大学交换生去巴黎留学，Parker 留在美国修读法律。相爱的情侣就此被硬生生地分开。那个时代还没有 facebook，他们只能靠书信，每写完一封信，都是漫长焦心的等待。Parker 为此痛苦不已。为了能在假期和心上人团聚，他省吃俭用地攒着机票钱。终于，他生平第一次站在了埃菲尔塔下，震撼他的除了出落得日益标致的 Pat，还有巴黎大街小巷里散发着的各式香草、巧克力、奶油的迷人香气。那天，他和 Pat 找了家餐厅吃饭，Pat 点了葡萄酒。从那杯酒开始，大鼻子找到了人生除了 Pat 以外的另一份真爱。

大鼻子没有懂酒的老爸做启蒙老师，全靠买书自学。他家里也没有祖上传下来的葡萄酒收藏，于是一次次地去葡萄酒商店淘便宜货。他渐渐发现自己的嗅觉和味觉天分，于是开始招募兄弟会成员成立品酒小组。后面的故事不用说也知道，他创立了那本足以改变世界葡萄酒格局的《葡萄酒倡导者》。

那本杂志之所以会在短时间内吸引大量拥护者和追随者，前所未有的全新葡萄酒语言和语气是 Parker 的重要筹码。

A former lawyer, Parker knows and doesn't care that he is considered "an uncultured American by some Europeans."

His 100-point rating system has been the biggest breakthrough in ending the European monopoly on wine reviews. His system is simple and effective - evaluating a wine from its appearance, nose, flavor and aging potential.

"When I look at the significances of what I've done in the last 32 years, it's probably been in having brought a democratic aspect to wine evaluation," he says. "I brought a very pro-consumer independent view."

His wine reviews, published in The Wine Advocate, have a loyal following. Often after the newsletter is published, the wines scoring over 90 sell out in a week. Few retailers want to carry wines scoring less than 81 points.

读者们普遍的感受是，这本杂志，就像是一个普通人写给普通人的。一切都显得公开透明，唾手可得。作者只是花了点时间替大家尝了一遍，这和先前任何一本持专家说教口气的读物不同。以 1982 年份波尔多为例，这个年份的酒评让他一战成名。他这样写道：这是个伟大的年份，趁现在价格不高多买一点，绝对是笔划算的投资。

每一款酒，他都写明自己的品尝方式，非常具体。对于波尔多的酒，他都会醒酒 3 个小时，并在酒杯中留那么一点，分别在 24 小时和 48 小时后再去品尝，从而判断酒的陈年潜力。

His preference for Bordeaux wines has been blamed for causing their prices to skyrocket in recent years. He has also been criticized as "singularizing the world's taste in wine" since more wine producers tend to make wines catering to his personal taste for dark, ripe and high-alcohol wines. People have called this the "Parkerization" of the wine world.

Parker himself doesn't like the word.

"It's a criticism and it's untrue," he says. "I don't think my taste can be defined so well that you could actually come up with the formula of what I like. If you examine all my writings, it's pretty clear that there's not one style."

"Good wine makers know their responsibility, producing natural wine to translate the personality and character of the vineyard and vintage without compromise," he adds.

"Changing their style to please one critic is a complete betrayal of their responsibility."

When Parker first started reviewing wines, most other wine writers were attached to the industry in some way or another.

They insisted on using an old approach to wine, focusing on hierarchies of chateaus and the story behind the bottle, not necessarily the liquid inside it.

He buys his own wine and does not accept gifts from wine traders.

从语言角度，大鼻子去掉了一贯以来欧洲人崇尚的抽象、笼统描述感官的词汇，最具代表性的莫过于"优雅""高贵""芬芳"这三滴万金油。Parker 创立了一套让读者产生共鸣的，具体、生动且严谨的语法体系。当描述口感的时候，他会使用稀松平常的材质和触感，比如"丝滑""天鹅绒般""有嚼劲""多汁""肉感""粘稠"等等。当描述香气和味道的时候，他可以具体到"生青的梨""熟透了的草莓做出来的果酱""培根上的那块脂肪""蛋糕上那层灌奶油"。偶尔，他也会用到些俏皮的字眼，比如用"水果炸弹"来表述果香四溢的新世界赤霞珠，用"液体版伟哥"来描述那种带有魅惑感的阳刚味道。

对一款酒作出结论的时候，他选择了连小学生都看得懂的百分制评分，一般分为七个区间，96 — 100，近乎完美；90 — 95，杰出作品；80 — 89，非常好；75 — 59，中等偏上；65 — 74，普通；60 — 64，有明显错误；64 以下，建议回避。采取 20 分制的 Jancis 觉得这样过于精准的评判体系给了 Parker 很大的主观空间。

"我尊重她是一个伟大的酒评家。这世上没有一套打分系统是完美的，但最起码我的百分制目前为止仍然是公正体现葡萄酒品质相对理想的工具。"Parker 为自己辩驳道。

随着 Parker 越来越出名，直到成为一个美国的传奇，围绕他的研究也越来越多。大鼻子闻到的那些香气是不是大家都能闻到呢？加州大学达沃斯分校教授 Adrienne Lehre 特意做了一次调查性试验，让每一个小组成员通过盲品写下对于香气和口感的体验，结果没有发现任何共性。问题来了，如果真是这样，大鼻子那么多坚定的追随者哪里来呢？

"我因为类似的原因失去了很多原本很要好的同事和朋友。但是，保持独立是获得读者信任的根本前提。乐观想想，这也变相迫使很多酒庄提升了自己葡萄酒的品质，也算是公德一件。"他大概是全世界唯一不接受酒商赞助，自掏腰包买酒的独立酒评家，他的杂志也不刊登任何商业广告。中国有句古话，吃人嘴软，拿人手短。既不吃又不拿，那还有什么不能说。

没有隐瞒，不惧权威，让他获得了公信力，也由此带给了他更大的话语权。他的分数既可以让一家不知名的新兴酒庄或是被忽略的小产区一夜成名，也足以让百年名庄顷刻间名誉扫地，陷入商品滞销，资金链断裂的万劫不复。他曾经公开质疑 1957 年份的波尔多一级庄普遍有被估值过高的嫌疑。但他也为此付出了一系列惨痛的代价。

有一年，Parker 在给法国圣爱美隆名庄白马庄打了低分后拜访酒庄。结果，他的膝盖被酒庄放出的一条狗咬伤。至今为止，他的名字仍然醒目地出现在很多欧洲酒庄的访客黑名单上。据说他还曾经因为给几款酒打低分而收到一个美国葡萄酒零售商的死亡威胁，幸运的是最终只是受了点伤。

人们说他身上这种正义感和他大学时期修读法律有着千丝万缕的关系。

In his world, famous wines such as Chateau Lafite Rothschild and Chateau Margaux are treated the same as any other wine. Before gaining notoriety, Parker started questioning the value of some wines from such chateaus, declaring some to be overrated.

And while he reviews many fine wines, he makes an effort to review many bottles that everyone can afford.

"I have a certain responsibility to the producer, but the ultimate is the wine consumer. It's them putting confidence in reading what I said," Parker says.

Over the years he has received at least one death threat (from a New York City retailer after he wrote a bad review) and he's been banned from some famous chateaus.

大鼻子的思路显现出和欧洲酒评家本质上的不同。多数英国或是法国的酒评家和葡萄酒行业关系紧密，无论是酒庄还是经销商，餐厅或是酒店。为行业背书，是他们得以生存的必要条件。

欧洲派的代表Jancis仍然没法认同大鼻子："我就是不明白了，如果不花时间和这个行业里的人相处，你又怎么能学到更多的葡萄酒知识呢？"

"I've lost sort of professional colleagues and friends because of that," he says. "However, an independent voice has value in giving people credibility. It also plays the role of pushing producers, letting them know they need to work harder to increase the quality of wine."

Parker's professional reviews are based on tasting around 10,000 wines a year. He says he can remember every great wine he has tasted, especially those "great wines" that are actually bad.

也对，Jancis 已获取了葡萄酒世界的最高学历"葡萄酒大师"；而大鼻子身上什么证书也没有。可就是因为这样，绝大部分身上没有证书的消费者才更加感同身受：这才是我们的 Parker！

大鼻子长期以来所表现出的以大众消费者为主导的那种草根英雄的形象全然不是扭捏作态。相当长的一段时间里，他都过着普通美国人的生活：开着辆国产车，痴迷于 NBA 联赛，听着 Bob Dylan 的歌，偶尔和 Pat 骑着自行车兜兜风。

不忘初心，方得始终。但愿 Parker 永远是我们的大鼻子。

"I wasn't a very good lawyer," says Parker. "But when it comes to wine, I have an extraordinary laser-like focus. That's just a matter of loving what I do.

"When tasting starts, it's like going into an alternative world. Everything in the glass, it's just me and that," he says.

Parker takes care of his nose and palate. He has given up espresso, garlic and chocolate so that his judgment is not impaired. He drinks mineral water often and takes vitamin C and ginseng to avoid catching a cold and getting congested.

With criticism and praise following him wherever he goes, Parker tries to keep level headed about it all.

"I know how good I am, how hard I work," he says. "I appreciate constructive criticism and prefer people saying: 'Parker, you need to reevaluate this wine.' Wine consumers now realize that no one is perfect. But if you're not influenced by wineries and say what you believe to be the truth from your heart, they will give you a lot of chances to make mistakes."

137/157

去精英化思维的
亚洲第一
葡萄酒拍卖师

香港人谭业明是佳士得中国区名酒部主管，也是佳士得拍卖行历史上第一个担任这个职位的中国人。他的英文名 Simon 更为人所熟知。

Hammering
out
fine wine details

谭业明随身携带的记事本里藏着亚洲那些顶级富豪的秘密。他们中有些人一夜暴富，急不可待地要找齐全世界最稀有最昂贵的葡萄酒来装备自己的酒窖。也有些人或因为家道中落，拿出祖父留给自己的最后那些值钱的葡萄酒来拍卖套现。

第一次见到 Simon 是 2013 年上海的一个夏夜。佳士得，这个源自英国的世界顶级拍卖行在中国大陆进行首拍。听说，毕加索的一幅画还有一条缅甸鸽血红宝石项链极有可能拍出天价。葡萄酒收藏家们则对当晚那瓶 1982 年的拉菲抱着势在必得的态度。拍卖会放在新落成的奢华酒店静安香格里拉。开始时间是晚上7 点，但从 5 点开始，酒店门口就聚集着大批保安，他们神色警觉地望着周边的一切。富豪买家们陆续到达，伴随着一辆比一辆惹眼的豪华座驾。路人都停下脚步窃窃私语，猜是来了什么大人物。

Simon 早早地站在拍卖台后面，时不时地望一眼台下，拿出手帕抹去额头上微微渗出的汗珠。记得他第一次做拍卖师时，也是差不多的场景，现场有一百来号人。他的目光紧紧地盯着台下的每一个人，生怕错过任何一次举牌和电话竞拍。上海的买家们每隔几秒都会举一次牌，价格正不断地被刷新。最终，那瓶 1982 年拉菲以 34 万起拍，以 45 万落槌。其他三件红酒拍品，包括一瓶 2000 年份大瓶装拉图都拍出了好价钱。这是他领导的名酒部在内地的一次成功且收获颇丰的试水。但 Simon 似乎开心不起来，眉宇中透着忧心忡忡。

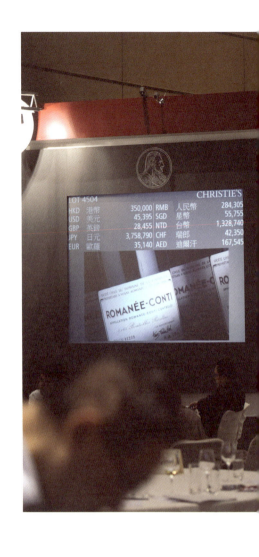

几个月前，他为香港前政务司司长、特区行政长官候选人唐英年举办了一次专场葡萄酒拍卖，堪称亚洲葡萄酒拍卖史上的一个奇迹，总成交额高达 4800 万港币，震动了全球葡萄酒收藏界。唐英年第一次展现了他大规模的勃艮第葡萄酒收藏，共 809 件佳酿，汇集了 71 家酒庄，跨越了从 1949 到 2010 年间的所有年份。其中 6 瓶 1995 年份的罗曼尼康帝更是拍出了 121 万的历史天价。可就在拍卖会结束后没几天，一名美国律师通过媒体公开质疑，认为这次拍卖的罗曼尼康帝酒款中，至少有 3 件是假货，理由

是那个年份产量极少，几乎在市面上已绝迹。最终，罗曼尼康帝的负责人站出来证明该酒经过验证的确产自他们酒庄。唐英年以诽谤为名向该律师提出起诉。（关于唐英年的葡萄酒人生，可以参看本书关于唐英年的专访）

假酒风波虽然被证明是子虚乌有，却触动了 Simon 职业生涯中最敏感的神经——信任，还有 provenance。

像唐英年这样的亚洲顶级收藏家之所以委托 Simon 来处理他的收藏，是因为他相信佳士得的专业能帮他卖个好价钱。而有钱人之所以到 Simon 的拍卖会上买酒，是相信佳士得的专业团队能确保他们买到的是真酒，且保存完好。毕竟葡萄酒要造假，不是那么难。制假可以非常粗糙，也可以做得非常精细，以假乱真到很多像 Jancis Robinson, Robert Parker 这样的酒评家也难以识别。比如被美国联邦调查局逮捕的美籍印度尼西亚裔 Rudy Kurniawan，当局在他位于加州的豪宅里发现他用高仿的波尔多和勃艮第名庄的酒瓶、酒标和橡木塞灌装美国加州的廉价酒。

这份存在于拍卖行和买家之间的信任可以达到什么样的高度？一瓶假酒，佳士得如果说是真的，那旁人也就认为是真的了。

Wine auctioneer Simon Tam focuses on gaining the trust of Chinese wine collectors through his dedication to provenance and making wine more accessible. Ruby Gao uncorks a bottle.

Asia's top wine auctioneer Simon Tam compares himself to a glass of Sherry Palo Cortado, old-fashioned yet delicious, and perhaps most importantly, it can age over a long time.

The Hong Kong-based auctioneer successfully co-hosted the wine section in Christie's first-ever Chinese mainland auction on September 26 in Shanghai. But he says he still cannot forget the first time he pounded the gavel down on the rostrum to conclude a sale. He was nervous, he recalls, his eyes darting around to make sure he didn't miss any bids from the 100 people in the room.

"When I said 'sold, yours,' my life's work had changed," Tam says.

"在我眼里，provenance 为王。如果没有好的 provenance，我宁愿不做这笔生意。" Simon 说得掷地有声。

他反复提到的那个英文单词 provenance 就是构筑拍卖行信誉的基石。

这个词源自法语，早年用于欧洲古董艺术品市场的交易，主要是指每一件艺术品从诞生之日起历经的每一任主人，被转手存放过的每一个仓库的历史凭证。我姑且把它翻译为生命的线索。

在追寻每一瓶酒生命线索的过程中，Simon 和他的团队扮演着一半侦探、一半历史学家的角色。

很多时候，他们的身影出现在欧洲古老而昏暗的地下酒窖。这些酒窖多设计成拱形，无论多么轻手轻脚，脚步声总会轻易地折射在墙壁上，发出长长的、令人有些害怕的回音。

那些沉睡了近半个世纪，或是更久的葡萄酒静静地躺在那里，或井然有序，或横七竖八。若是主人平时疏于照顾，上面都结着一层又一层的灰，有时还夹杂着乱成一团的蜘蛛网。

Big auction houses are the preferred choice among wine lovers seeking to buy rare wines because they trust the auctioneer's professionalism. Such auctions also often provide the best wines at the best prices.

Being a salesman is part of the job and the part that is most noticeable. However, most of his work is done before the auction. This includes finding clients who want to sell part of their wine collection and assessing and cataloguing the wines that will be sold.

A wine auctioneer is known for assessing the value of a wine without tasting it, and using a distinctive language to write the catalogue.

Gaining trust among collectors is not easy. The auctioneer needs to rely on deep knowledge of wines and vineyards, yet they also have to be somewhat of a detective to check that wines have been stored properly to ensure quality.

"Even though it seems that my job is always about 50,000-yuan (US$8,064.5) bottles of Lafite 1920 and 1990, knowledge is far more important," Tam tells Shanghai Daily during an exclusive interview in Hong Kong.

"那些糟透了的酒窖很多都在欧洲，我曾看到过最惨不忍睹的：木箱破了，酒从里面漏出来，而且没有任何恒温装置。" Simon 回忆道。

倒是亚洲收藏家的酒窖，多半非常考究。主人会在豪宅里辟一块最合适的区域，借助科技手段，为这些酒创造完美的储存温度、湿度和光线。红、白、气泡分区域摆放。每块区域又细分为各个产地，再细分到酒庄，最后细分到年份。有些亚洲收藏家偏执到一定要把他喜爱酒庄的所有年份收齐才罢手。

"这很容易解释。亚洲收藏家的酒都是他们不惜重金买来品尝的，自然格外珍惜。相反的，欧洲收藏家的酒很多都是来自遗产继承或是朋友间的赠予，也就比较随便了。" Simon 说道。

A large role in Christie's wine sales

Tam, 45, was born in Hong Kong, but moved to Australia with his parents when he was eight years old. He returned to his birthplace in 1992, and is now "the first and only Chinese head of an international auction house's wine department."

He joined Christie's two years ago and has played a large role in the auction house's increasing wine sales in Asia, which have been largely driven by Chinese bidders. Before that, he founded the Independent Wine Center, a wine education and consulting organization with offices in both Hong Kong and Shanghai.

According to Christie's, the number of Chinese wine bidders has increased 1,550 percent from 2008 to 2012, when Hong Kong eliminated duties on wine, bringing prices down.

Tam attributes his success to his commitment to perfect provenance and his understanding of Chinese and Western cultures.

"For me, my job is to bring the best provenance to auction. If I have any suspicion, I just turn it out of the cellar," Tam says.

Provenance refers to a record of ownership and is crucial in determining whether a wine has been properly stored.

随着那些老酒年代愈发久远，而全球的葡萄酒收藏人群日益庞大复杂，要找到够资格拍卖的酒愈发艰难。

Simon 的团队戴上手套，拿出放大镜和手电筒开始工作。团队成员名片上都印着"佳士得葡萄酒专家"。

顶级葡萄酒的购买和交易多以箱为单位。若是存放超过 20 年，就必须开箱检查。他们主要看的是酒瓶内液面的高低。

放久了，瓶中的酒就会透过橡木塞中细微的空隙与外界的空气接触，于是产生微妙而缓慢的变化。新鲜的果香逐渐褪去，更复杂深沉的陈年香气一层一层地铺展开来。酒评家们经常会用到花瓣、野味、松露、皮革、湿树叶这样的字眼去形容这些味道。这样的变化被公认为一瓶老酒最美妙的地方。与此同时，酒液也会不可避免地遭受不同程度的蒸发，从而使瓶中的液面降低。

Simon 会看同一箱里每一瓶酒的液面高低是否保持一致。如果相互之间差异不大就表明储存环境的温度和湿度相对稳定，酒的品质仍然良好。但若是液面差异大，酒的拍卖价值就有待商榷了。

He says Chinese collectors are often more demanding about provenance than Westerners because Chinese buy wine to drink. As the top auctioneer, Tam probably visits the most wine cellars in Asia and he has found that Asian collectors generally store wine at near-perfect conditions.

He recalls finding some "amazingly bad cellars with broken wooden cases with wine dripping out and no air conditioning" among Western collectors. He says it's most likely because some Western collectors received the bottles as gifts. Thus finding a wine with great provenance is becoming increasingly difficult.

Tam says that's why only four lots of wine sold in Christie's first Chinese mainland auction, much less than art and jewelry pieces.

在无法开瓶检验的条件限制下，瓶口的酒帽，橡木塞上的记号，瓶身上的酒标是他们判断真假最直接的依据，因为每个酒庄在不同时期的装瓶都会带有该年代特有的历史标记。

"要读懂这些细节，你不仅要懂酒，还要熟读历史。" Simon 强调。

他用一瓶 1983 年的勃艮第葡萄酒举例。当年，同一酒庄生产的同批次的葡萄酒却被贴上各种新旧不一的酒标在市面上流通。

"如果对那段历史有深刻的了解，你就不会武断地将那些酒标不一致的老酒划定为赝品。事实上，当时勃艮第产区的葡萄酒生产商都是不谙世事非常朴素的农民。他们为了节省，有什么标就贴什么标。" Simon 进一步地解释道。

有些时候，即使所有的客观证据都指向是真品，佳士得那些经验丰富的专家的直觉却给出了个相反的答案。他们会把酒瓶送交工艺品专家检验，通过玻璃的材质和工艺去推断这瓶酒的年龄。有时他们会求助于字迹专家去分析酒标上的字体和印刷方式，从而推断是否为特定年代的产物。

"Those four lots were directly from the cellars of chateaux Lafite, Latour, Margaux and Mouton, which can be seen as perfect provenance. The final selling prices, around 20 percent more than estimated, were not crazy but good. Chinese wine lovers who are experienced and knowledgeable stop bidding at a reasonable price," the auctioneer says.

Tam shares his checklist for authenticating the provenance of a wine. It starts with asking the consigner to provide photos of the wine cellar, wine label and ullage. If they pass the check, a wine specialist is assigned to inspect the cellar in person.

A wooden case of wine is opened if it's older than 20 years. If the ullage of each bottle in the case is average, the wine is believed to have been stored properly. Varying ullage indicates the wine has not been stored at the proper temperature.

The auctioneer's team then starts looking for signs if anyone changes the wine inside. The capsule, cork and label are key indicators.

即使上述的检验流程全部顺利通过，Simon 仍不会把它拿出来卖。

"这只能证明酒当下的状况。我们仍然不能确定这批酒在上一个主人那里被怎样对待，或许已是十年前的事情了。" Simon 说道。

他的团队会像福尔摩斯那样抽丝剥茧，寻找更多证据去证明它的每一段过去。如果证据不充分，Simon 会果断放弃。

"这也就是为什么这次上海拍卖只有四批次的酒品。他们都是直接从拉菲、拉图、木桐、玛歌四大酒庄的酒窖运来，没有转手过。这样的 provenance 堪称完美！" Simon 说到这里，脸上不经意地流露出一丝骄傲。

从这一点看，Simon 一点都不像唯利是图的商人，更像是个作风严谨的学者。也没错，在担任佳士得名酒部主管之前，他在香港创办了 Independent Wine Center，致力于葡萄酒教育和咨询长达 20 年。

The capsule should match the label. The foil design needs to match the chateau's style at the time of bottling. A flashlight is used to inspect the cork and the marks on it.

The wine label to a large extent challenges an auctioneer's knowledge.

"It's much more complex than what wine lovers imagine," says Tam.

He cites 1983 Burgundy wine as an example. There are different labels for the same vintage — some old, some new. This doesn't mean the authenticity of the wine is doubted necessarily.

"Many Burgundy wine producers are old-fashioned farmers, who stick the label on the bottle freely for not wasting anything. But the physical check only ensures the current storage environment of the wine, we cannot tell how it was treated 10 years ago. Thus, we will ask the consigner to provide the receipt and record of each bottle and check the source," Tam adds.

If he is not satisfied with the provenance, he gives up the business.

有意思的是，这样秉持原则的处事方式丝毫没有影响 Simon 为佳士得贡献利润。根据佳士得提供的数据，从 2008 年，唐英年废除香港葡萄酒关税之日开始到 2012 年，佳士得的中国买家数量增长了 1550%。

这样的成绩和 Simon 的跨文化背景密不可分。Simon 今年 47 岁，出生于香港，8 岁随父母移居澳洲。他的父母在澳洲拥有 20 家中餐馆。为了继承家业，他考取了当地的 Regency College 学习旅游管理和葡萄酒市场营销。24 岁那年他回到香港发展。

一方面，扎实的西方背景让他与欧美酒庄的沟通零障碍。另一方面，身为一个中国人，他更懂中国人。这句话的更深层含义潜藏在 Simon 的那本拍卖名录里。

One of Tam's claims to fame is that his China specialist team at Christie's introduced "Perfect Pairings" in the wine catalogues of spring auction this May. It aims to promote Chinese and other Asian dining cultures as well as to encourage wine collectors to explore drinking pleasure matched with food.

After all, serving steak with wine is not part of Chinese daily life, Tam says. Peking roast duck with a Burgundy red, and hairy crab roe meatballs with a 1988 vintage Champagne are his two "golden" pairings.

He has also worked hard to cultivate his own writing style that is simple and readable. Tam avoids terms such as "chocolate flavor" or "smells of cinnamon" that are often used by wine critics.

One Tam wine description reads: "The soft and fruity wine brings you a feeling of happiness and makes me think of my good old friend. If my father was still alive, I would definitely open the bottle with him."

"只有亲和平实的语言才有打动人心的力量。把葡萄酒形容成一种记忆，那才是品酒的最高境界。"这是 Simon 的品酒之道。

在佳士得举办每场拍卖会之前，它的 VIP 客户都会收到一本装帧精美的目录别册，上面罗列着每一件拍品的信息。翻开由 Simon 主编的那本，上面写着这样一段话：

"修道院红颜容堪称与一级酒庄并驾齐驱。一位备受推崇的品酒师曾经形容其葡萄酒为行家眼中的至尊极品，很少有酒庄能如修道院红颜容一般，连白葡萄酒也令人惊艳。"

看到这里，Simon 的语言与任何一家拍卖行或是酒商没什么不同。可他紧接着话锋一转：

"潮州手打牛丸是相当具有人气的街头小吃，弹性十足且相当有嚼劲。最地道的手打牛丸落到地上可以像乒乓球一样反弹跳动。搭配经典的梅多克干红，可以算是绝配。赤霞珠强劲的丹宁，搭配美乐柔顺的果香，与牛肉是天生的好朋友。"

将每一款酒与中国美食进行搭配，在佳士得历史上算是开天辟地了。街头小吃和顶级名庄碰撞出的火花更使葡萄酒超越了文化与价格的边界。

His writing adds emotion and personality to wine descriptions. Tam attributes it to working as a wine educator, teaching wine beginners about his passion in a fun way.

Jonathan Fewtrell, a former wine student of Tam's, says: "Simon impresses by using plain language, avoiding waffle and demonstrating some simple and surprisingly effective techniques ... that even a novice like me can take away and use in real life."

A people person

Tam says his knack for describing wine in memorable words is due to building a relationship between wine and occasion, wine and memory.

"That's the highest stage of appreciating wine," the auctioneer says.

"Besides the salary, it's people that keep me going. I love interaction, which helps me learn new things," he says.

"我们要让葡萄酒真正意义上走入国人的生活。毕竟牛排和红酒的组合不是中国人生活中的主题。" Simon 强调。

As a wine auctioneer, he feels lucky because most people enjoy a good wine.

Seeking out potential clients is often, well, a wining and dining process. If one of his clients opens a bottle of wine, four or five of his friends are invited to have a glass. These friends then become potential clients.

他的这一想法和早年投身教育时开发的一个名叫 Flavour Colours 的应用程序有关。这是个基于中国孔老夫子"不时不食"思想而建立的餐酒搭配体系。Simon 把所有的食物和美酒划分为亚麻金、象牙白、茶色、深咖啡四个颜色，对应春夏秋冬四个季节。食物的季节性不言而喻，而酒的季节色彩则是 Simon 赋予的。比如说，那些带有柠檬，淡雅小白花香气的长相思，或是年轻的雷司令让人联想到明媚的春光，又比如那些深沉却又不那么浓烈的顶级勃艮第和年份香槟让人联想到缤纷、丰收的秋日。由此，中国人不一定要通晓像丹宁、酸度、酒体那样的专业词汇，可以直接按季节和颜色进行餐酒搭配。

到了拍卖现场，Simon 作为拍卖师又有一套自成一派的语言体系：

"这是一款让人产生幸福感的酒，那么柔软，果香四溢。如果我爸爸还活着，我一定会当着他的面打开它！"

Simon 有意识地删去了些晦涩难懂，估计只有酒评家才会使用的字眼，像雪松、骨架、收尾长度。Simon 这样的去精英化思维，从某种程度上说，很不佳士得。这家由 James Christie 在 1766 年创立的拍卖行以艺术品交易起家，在近 250 年里一直努力地维持着一种高冷的姿态。

佳士得的中国总部位于香港中环的历山大厦。这位置相信是精挑细选的，大厦的一边是上流社会云集的文华东方酒店，另一边是地标性的精品百货店——置地广场，土豪的乐园。

采访 Simon 的时间正值每年最具分量的秋拍前夕。他的同事强烈推荐我去旁听一场为艺术拍品而举办的讲座，地点就在历山大厦。来听讲的客人看上去极为体面和优雅，穿戴的都是名牌中的限量款。主持讲座的佳士得艺术品专家是个英国人，他正如痴如醉地描述着一幅画中每一个细腻笔触背后所隐藏的含义，但一点也不夸张，他那双深邃的眼睛长在了头顶上。正当我听得入迷的时候，一个保安把我拉开，说了句：离画作远一点。

Compared with art and jewelry auctioneers, whose clients are dominated by millionaires and billionaires, Tam's clients are much more diverse because many fine wines are affordable.

"For the Henry Tang (Asia's biggest wine collector) wine auction as an example, some of the bottles sold for 2,500 yuan. You don't need to be a millionaire, you just need a passion for wine," Tam says.

His sense of achievement mainly comes from selling unknown inexpensive wines, not the famous first-growth Bordeaux vintages. People buying the former have confidence and faith in him and those buying the later have more confidence in labels.

Asked about his favorite wine memory, Tam says he enjoys the time with his father-in-law every year he goes to Portugal with his Portuguese wife.

"I play a wine game with him. We have a competition to see who can identify the most cost-effective wine," he recalls. "Usually he wins because he's local."

Simon 认为这样的差异是由葡萄酒的本质决定的。艺术和珠宝部门的客户，无一例外是千万或是亿万富翁。但名酒部则不同，除了那些顶级名庄会被拍出天价，多数拍品是普通葡萄酒爱好者负担得起的。

"就拿唐英年专场拍卖举例好了，有些酒也就卖 1500 元人民币一瓶。有钱并不是爱酒喝酒的充要条件。"Simon 说道。

他工作中最大的成就感并非来自那些天价成交的名庄酒，而是成交了那些好喝又不贵的酒。

"很简单，人们买前者是因为相信酒标上的名字，而买后者是出于对我专业上的信任。"他解释。

性价比，在 Simon 看来是最有意思的葡萄酒课题。他的太太是葡萄牙人。每年他最期待的就是回葡萄牙和岳父玩一场葡萄酒的游戏：

"我们会各自去找酒，然后比赛谁的性价比高。不过，通常是他赢，谁让他是当地人呢！"

言下之意，要是这比赛挪到了中国，Simon 赢得妥妥的。

这样的葡萄酒理念让 Simon 交友广阔。每天从中午到晚上，都有无数场饭局等着他。这样的应酬，恐怕是个人都会心生向往，甚至嫉妒的。饭局的由头多数情况下是谁又觅到了好酒，也可能是得来不易的珍贵食材，比如一份上好的和牛，一大块皮尔蒙特白松露。"干杯""cheers""tchin tchin"之后，一笔生意也达成了，因为肯花钱花时间认真吃喝的人，八九不离十，藏着个极为精彩的酒窖。

"你看我，最近又胖了！"Simon 笑着抱怨道。

其实他很享受这样的工作状态。人在最熟悉的氛围和环境里是最放松，最具安全感的。在餐厅里交朋友是他儿时的生活常态。

我问他，什么样的酒最能表达你的心情，个性和目前为止人生的的全部？

他说是那杯 Palo Cortado 的雪利酒，称不上时髦，但绝对好喝。更重要的是，经得起陈年。

Simon 的思绪回到小时候。那一年，他 16 岁，是他和葡萄酒的初恋，一段"偷来"的真爱。

他父母开在澳洲的中餐厅酒柜里陈列着一排一排的好酒。澳洲本来就是个出酒的好地方，当地人也习惯用餐的时候来上一杯，即使是吃中餐。

有一天，他妈妈开了瓶 1961 年的拉菲，一边喝，一边赞不绝口，脸上写着种 Simon 极少见到的心满意足。

"我就把剩下来的半瓶偷过来和小伙伴们分享。奇怪了，为什么被妈妈视为天籁的酒我们喝起来都觉得一般，甚至是不好喝。我想知道这么大的区别背后到底藏着怎样的秘密，在寻找答案的过程中也就爱上了葡萄酒。" Simon 回忆道。

现在的他最想偷的是时间。一天 24 小时根本不够用。

Tam traces his affection for people back to his childhood.

His family owned 20 Chinese restaurants in South Australia, so he was often around large groups enjoying a nice meal. To help his family business, he studied hospitality management and wine marketing at Regency and Roseworthy Colleges in Australia.

At the age of 16, he stole half a bottle of 1961 Chateau Lafite from his mother.

"Mom said the wine is amazing. I shared the bottle with my friends and we all thought it was not very tasty. I was curious why we had such different opinions," the auctioneer says.

This was his start into the wine world.

Tam says he is so busy that he wishes there were 35 hours in a day. During the day he handles Christie's wine fairs in Asia; in the evening he contacts Christie's London and New York offices as well as Western wine producers.

"我恨不得一天有35个小时！"Simon 边说边摇着头。

翻开他的行事历，真不敢相信这紧凑到已经是血淋淋的工作节奏。白天，他既要管理香港的整个团队，又要和大陆地区的买家和合作伙伴进行沟通和协商。到了晚上，因为时差关系，他经常要和伦敦和纽约地区的卖家电话、邮件到深夜。

这点时间对于达成他心中正酝酿的那些宏伟计划来说，太有限了。

他想在大陆地区举办更多场次的葡萄酒拍卖，借这样的机会把最好的酒呈现给这块庞大且日益增长的市场。可关税、物流都是有待逾越的障碍。他想建立一套更为完善的 provenance 追溯体系来获得买家的信任，让类似唐英年被质疑卖假酒这样的噩梦不再重演。

"我真希望能早点达成这些个梦想，但没有什么能一步到位，只能细水长流。等待的过程，有时真的很痛苦，很挣扎。"Simon 说道。

Simon 或许低估了自己经受时间考验的能力。至于他口袋里那本富豪笔记本里的秘密，他一个字也不肯说。

He's planning to hold more wine auctions on the Chinese mainland. He's also trying to establish a proper provenance checking system to gain more trust from Chinese wine lovers.

He also runs an iPhone application "Flavour Colours," arguably the first Chinese food and wine pairing app.

Tam is an active wine columnist and speaker at various wine conferences.

"Time is very important for us to continue telling the story of wine in China," he says.

Luckily, time seems to be on his side as sherry is known to age rather well.

Simon Talks about 'Flavour Colours'

It's an app showing my wine philosophy, categorizing food and wine into four colours — blond, ivory, tan and brown.

Color does not just represent flavor but also seasonality. Chinese don't always choose food and wine because of certain flavors, but because of weather.

For example, blond brings to mind the zest of fresh lemon, delicate white flower blossoms and a sunny day with sea breezes. Brown represents warmth, a sense of comfort represented by a mature old red, and dark chocolate truffles. I take away technical and complicated language and use color matching to make food and wine pairing easier to understand.

1. 苏富比拍卖行

2. 北京保利国际拍卖有限公司

3. 上海国际商品拍卖有限公司

大中华地区葡萄酒拍卖行

一个美国
葡萄酒进口商
如何做到中国第一

世界上，有些人生来就是要成为企业家的。

他们像是非洲原始丛林中的猎豹，能在腥风血雨中生存。猎物时，他们反应极快，快到你根本不知道谁是下一个目标。ASC 精品酒业创始人 Don St Pierre Jr 就是这样的一个人。

Wine
importer
turns
problems
into pluses

Don 的办公室位于十八楼，窗外看得到黄浦江以西迷人的天际线。46 岁的他穿着淡粉色印花衬衫和白色长裤，在一群西装革履的员工中显得惹眼。这符合他的新角色，从 2012 年开始，Don 不再担任 CEO，升任公司董事局主席。

对于这个变动，Don 解释道，这个世界上有两种人，一种是打天下的企业家，他们富有冒险精神，敢于做梦和创新。另一种是守天下的职业经理人，用严谨的态度确保在一个庞大的商业帝国中，每一个零件都能很好地运转。

"我明显属于前者。"他笑言。

今日的 ASC 已是中国最大的葡萄酒进口商，代理了超过 1200 个来自全球 14 个国家的品牌，拥有上千名员工。Robert Parker，全球最负盛名的酒评家用 "greatest（最伟大的）" 来评价 ASC 在中国的影响力。很多人好奇，甚至嫉妒，一个连中文都不会说的美国人凭什么就做了中国的葡萄酒老大？

AMERICAN Don St Pierre Jr, co-founder of leading wine importer ASC Fine Wines, knows from difficult personal experiences how to turn a problem into an opportunity and turn his company into a major force in the fine wine market.

The 46-year-old executive chairman of the board of ASC compares himself to a glass of Chateau Latour.

"It is long lasting and always perseveres to make a great wine even in the most difficult years," he tells Shanghai Daily.

ASC is headquartered in Shanghai and represents more than 1,200 wines from 14 countries. It was founded 18 years ago in Beijing by Don St Pierre Sr, now retired, and the junior St Pierre.

The most difficult year was 2008 when St Pierre Jr was detained in Shanghai for 28 days, charged with attempted tax evasion by undervaluing the wine he declared to customs, due to his misunderstanding of taxation regulations on China's mainland. However, St Pierre Jr admitted the charges and paid duties amounting to 1.8 million yuan (US$290,000).

"在中国的无数个夜晚，种种的困难和障碍都让我产生强烈的挫败感。但第二天早晨醒来，我仍保持着一颗强大的心，坚定地走下去。" Don 望了望窗外。

Speaking of that experience, he says, "It's hard. You have to have self-belief to go through it. But we turned a problem into an opportunity finally."

Two years later, ASC established guanxi (connections) with the Chinese government, becoming its primary option for consulting, especially on the global price of wines as a reference for customs officials looking for tax evasion.

In turn, ASC, the exclusive distributor of DBR Lafite, owner of Chateau Lafite, has benefited by the government crackdown on counterfeit Lafite bottles.

Tax evasion and smuggling are the biggest challenges faced by China's fine wine industry and they will continue as long as high taxes on value, not volume, remain unchanged, St Pierre Jr says.

他相信自己就是那杯 Chateau Latour（拉图庄），持久而坚韧，即使是最差的年份，也能绝处逢生，酿造出伟大的佳酿。

2008 是 Don 人生中最黑暗的一年。三月的一天，他如往常一样被司机接去上班，但一直到晚上，他都没有出现在公司，也没有回家，好像是人间蒸发。家人同事陷入了恐慌，直到被告知 Don 涉嫌偷税漏税，操纵进口价格，被中国海关扣留。Don 的爸爸，ASC 的联合创始人，绝望中向海关展示了他和中国前总理朱镕基的合影，自然没有任何效果。二十八天后，他被放了出来，ASC 承认漏税，向海关交还了 180 万人民币。

"这二十八天对我真的是一种折磨，如果心里缺了份坚定的信念，根本就没法撑下去。但，我把这次的危难转化成了一个大机遇！"Don 回忆道。

两年后，ASC 成为了中国海关的首席合作伙伴，帮助海关人员进行葡萄酒专业培训，并为其提供进口葡萄酒的全球浮动价格。海关以此为主要参照依据来判断进口商是否为避税而瞒报了进口价格。与此同时，ASC 作为拉菲所属母公司 DBR 拉菲的中国独家代理商, 也从中国政府一系列打击假酒，尤其是假拉菲的行动中大大受益。

Speaking of smuggling, he says most takes place between Hong Kong, which charges zero duty on wine imports, and Shenzhen in Guangdong Province, where tax is applied to value, not volume.

"Smuggling, though recently going down due to the anti-corruption drive, is still serious and will continue for a very long time unless the current tax structure on China's mainland is changed," he says.

In countries like the United States and Singapore, wine import duties are applied to volume, but when it is applied to value, importers have a big incentive to falsify value.

The taxation on China's mainland forced the company to open offices in Hong Kong.

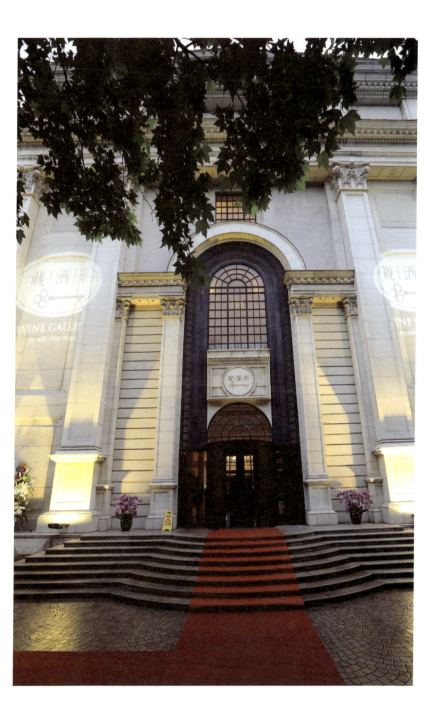

直至今日，偷税和走私问题仍然是中国葡萄酒产业中的一颗毒瘤，丝毫没有减弱的势头。最严重的走私存在于香港（向进口葡萄酒征收零关税）和深圳之间，这大大困扰着 Don 和其他进口商。他不得不在香港设立分公司，从源头上堵住他所代理的品牌通过走私进入中国市场的可能性。

Don 认为滋养这颗毒瘤的是中国现行的税收体系，制度一天不改，走私一日不除。中国海关按进口产品的价值征税，而葡萄酒却是一个缺乏硬性价值衡量标准的产品。一款葡萄酒的生产成本很低，但价格浮动的空间却很大。酒庄的历史和出身，甚至酒评家对其主观的评价都左右着其市场价格。这使得进口商有机可乘，操纵价格。他强烈建议中国能参考美国或是新加坡的现行葡萄酒关税制度，按量征税，这是相对而言最为透明公正的。

2014 又是个充满动荡的一年。自中国国家主席习近平采取一系列反腐败措施，尤其是限制"三公消费"之后，喝拉菲、拉图的人少了很多，高端葡萄酒产业损失惨重。ASC 首当其中，放在 Don 面前的报表触目惊心，公司顶级葡萄酒的销售额最少下降了 30%。

"If I'm going to control the distribution of the brand on the mainland, I have to control how the brand is imported to Hong Kong or other companies may ship the wine to the mainland through smuggling," the importer explains.

Another challenge is China's anti-extravagance drive that has reduced lavish banquets and gifts of expensive wine. The austerity campaign has reduced sales of ASC's top expensive wines by at least 30 percent since the drive started, St Pierre Jr says.

He wants to seize this opportunity to expanding e-commerce since customers' consuming logic is changing: There is less buying of costly, prestigious label wines to impress officials and win favors and more buying of wines that people enjoy personally.

"但我仍然有信心将危难转化为机遇，就像当年一样。" Don 说道。

他早已开始布局葡萄酒电商领域，抢占个人消费者。电商更迎合新一代葡萄酒消费者的思维。当公务消费的需求减弱，人们买酒不再是为了讨好他人，而是取悦自己。

Americans St Pierre Jr and Don St Pierre Sr are probably the most successful fine wine importers in China. Wine critic Robert Parker has called ASC "China's greatest fine wine importer."

ASC is widely regarded as the wine industry's Whampoa Military Academy for nurturing talent. The academy produced distinguished commanders in World War II. For example, Simon Wang, now CEO of Kerry Wines, was vice president of sales of ASC; Martin Hao, now a Master of Wine candidate and leading wine educator, worked for ASC.

St Pierre Sr founded the company with his son in 1996. At that time, most of their rivals were in Hong Kong, but ASC's message to brands was that they were on the ground in China, hence, in the best position to do business.

Before retirement, St Pierre Sr was based in Beijing, handling operation in northern China. St Pierre Jr was (and still is) based in Shanghai and oversaw the south.

The senior St Pierre, who had once dreamed of being a baseball player, arrived in China in 1985. He was president of Beijing Jeep, the American-Sino Motors joint venture. At one time he was probably the single best-known businessman working in China.

"父亲告诉过我作为一个老外在中国的两条生存法则。第一，坚持不懈。第二，了解中国式思维。"Don 回忆道。

Don 坦陈，他的信心和勇气很大程度上来自于他的父亲 Don St Pierre Sr。父子两个名字过于相似，又同为公司创始人，行业内人为避免混淆，称呼父亲为大 Don，儿子为小 Don。

大 Don 在中国改革开放初期就已是个大人物，这从前文提到的他和中国领导人的合影中也不难看出来。早在 1985 年，他就来到北京，后来成为了中美合资北京吉普的董事长。美国媒体曾评价他为在中国最具影响力的美国商人。中国这块古老的土地孕育出了自己的一套思维模式和行事风格。Don 深知，"中国模式"四个字远比葡萄酒更有商业价值。这从他的管理团队也看得出来：首席执行官 John Watkins 在中国工作了近 30 年，开拓了通用和西北航空的中国市场。副总裁 Stephane Moreau 在中国的家乐福和百安居工作了近 20 年。

"He taught me to be competitive and to persevere," says his son.

His father also taught him the importance of understanding China's distinctive business ethic and logic.

"One of the reasons why we're successful is that we know about China more than the wine business," says St Pierre Jr.

CEO John Watkins, who worked for GE and Northwest Airlines, has more than 30 years' experience building business in China. Vice President Stephane Moreau, who worked for Carrefour and B&Q, has almost 20 years China experience.

"In China, I don't think you will be successful if you're only looking at the competition. You have to look at where the market's going and try to stay in front of that," St Pierre Jr explains.

中国经济发展虽然起步较晚，但也因此具备了一个新兴市场的活力和潜质。因而，敢于第一个吃螃蟹的人就是赢家！2006年，ASC成为中国第一个提供全球权威葡萄酒课程WSET的教育机构。

"一切从零开始，没有消费者我就培养消费者，没有专业从业人员，我就通过培训去创造！"Don解释道。

Don的努力得到了回报，虽然这份回报里伴随着一些令他伤心的回忆。ASC被很多人奉为中国葡萄酒产业的黄埔军校。公司曾经的销售副总裁Simon Wang现如今是嘉里酒业的首席执行官。知名葡萄酒作家、教育家郝利文，曾经为ASC效力。

"我最遗憾的就是那些本不应该离开我的人最终仍然选择了离开。年轻时，我曾为此而难过，但现在也想通了。在美国，有这么一句谚语，围栏另一边的草更绿。"他说道，眼睛里透出一丝藏不住的失落。

中国人生活中的一些细节，多多少少折射出另一种中国特色。人们不爱排队，火车站经常是一片混乱，马路上司机争相变道。赚钱也是一样，这里的商人不爱遵守游戏规则，最终拿到钱就是王道。

Don 采取的应对之策就是强有力的控制，甚至是垄断。ASC 与葡萄酒品牌的合作中，很大部分是拿下独家代理权。截至现在，他已是 DBR 拉菲、罗兰百悦、路易霞都、奔富等上百个品牌的中国独家代理商。

In 2006, ASC became the first provider of WSET (Wine and Spirit Education Trust) courses in China to cultivate customers by educating them. Four years later, it opened China's first licensed fine wine auction company. It is one of the first importers

他解释道，在中国，如果你不控制整个上下游资源，就意味着当你花了大量人力物力去经营某个葡萄酒品牌，完善他的销售渠道，增加他在消费者中的知晓度时，其他投机的进口商或正忙于借这个品牌套现获利，甚至不惜毁掉它的声誉和未来。

能拿下独家代理，多亏了他和父亲的内地优先策略。据 Don 说，早年多数的葡萄酒进口商都驻扎在香港。他们对品牌的说辞是，我们会兼顾内地市场。唯有 ASC 毅然决然地说，我们是驻扎在内地的进口商，内地是我们的全部。他和父亲非常清楚，借香港试水再打入内地市场的路线根本行不通，这是两块截然不同的土地。

to invite leading winery owners from abroad to talk with Chinese consumers.

"In this country, you have to control (the source)," St Pierre Jr says.

St Pierre Jr observes that in China local businessmen usually pursue the profit regardless of following rule.

"Anybody can import the product, though illegally, and operate a brand less professionally. That means ASC's investment in brands is meaningless if there's no exclusivity," he says.

Many wine importers in China are owned by big companies specializing in medical equipment, construction and real estate, he says, emphasizing that ASC is devoted exclusively to wine.

It is the exclusive distributor for DBR Lafite, Louis Jadot, Penfolds and Laurent Perrier, among others.

St Pierre Jr grew up in Ontario, Canada, attended school in Indonesia and lived in Hong Kong and Taipei for years. He can speak fairly good Mandarin.

Before going into wine, the father and son looked into infant care products, publishing, photocopying, even munitions.

In May 1995, their warehouse in California was investigated by the FBI for allegedly importing banned munitions from China. But the authorities dropped the case 5 weeks later.

父子间的争吵从来没有断过。Don 笑称，要不是他俩分隔在不同的城市，这父子关系没准会破裂。

十八年前，大 Don 和小 Don 决定在异国他乡携手创业，这是个艰难的决定。在做葡萄酒之前，他们曾涉猎过传媒、婴儿用品等其他行业，均以失败告终。他们终于意识到，老外在中国创业没有任何先天优势，但葡萄酒是个例外。这里的人理所当然地认为，那些碧眼金发的人更懂葡萄酒。

父子两人同为 ASC 老板，公司里，到底谁听谁的？这个问题，似乎从来就没有个答案。

父亲更看重投入资金的短期回报，儿子更看重长远利益。父亲不太能接受儿子花相当一部分"冤枉钱"去拓展维护各种合作关系。比如，ASC 会赞助一系列帮助在中国普及葡萄酒文化，培养葡萄酒人才的活动，包括每年一届的中国侍酒师大赛，酒评家 Jancis Robinson 撰写的葡萄酒教育类读物的中文版发行。"幸运的是，几乎我们所有的矛盾

They decided on wine because of their personal interest, social network and China's market potential.

Foreign entrepreneurs have an advantage in the wine business in China because wine drinking is perceived as a Western lifestyle, St Pierre Jr says.

They made many mistakes, underestimating the difficulty of running a business in China and how much money they would have to invest.

Father and son were frequently at odds while at the same time being good friends.

"My father was more focused on the short-term survival of the business while I was more focused on the long-term investments to build relationships," says St Pierre Jr.

He says with a laugh that it's a good thing that father and son worked in different cities, Beijing and Shanghai, or there would be more friction.

都能最终达成共识，并促成一个更合理妥善的方案，除了，"他停了停，"公司总部的选址。"

大 Don 坚持北京，因为这是中国政治中心。小 Don 坚持上海，认为这不仅是中国的经济中心，更是对西方文化最为包容的城市。两人都不愿妥协，结果父子各占一方，父亲常驻北京，负责北方市场，儿子常驻上海，负责东南方市场。相当长的一段时间，ASC 都没有明确其中国总部，一直到大 Don 退休，总部才正式设在了上海。

ASC undertakes many activities to promote interest in wine. It sponsors the China Sommelier Competition, publishes its own wine magazine about the latest trends and has financed the Chinese translation of critic Jancis Robinson's latest wine book "Jancis Robinson's Wine Course" and previously "World Atlas of Wines."

The company's turning point came in 2012, when Watkins replaced St Pierre Jr as CEO, signifying a move from family management to professional management. The company has 20-plus offices and about 1,100 staff.

当被问及人生最骄傲的时刻，很意外，Don 并没有提及他的事业，而是他第一个孩子的出生。

"我大女儿出生时那种初为人父的感觉，太难用语言来形容了。"眼前这头豹子说着，眼神瞬间温柔起来。

他和他的上海太太 Monica Xu 在一次品酒会上相识，生了三个女儿，Caitlyn, Ciana 和 Cailie。不再担任 CEO 后，他也有更多的时间来陪伴家庭。他说，女儿是他前进最大的动力。

ASC 已是中国进口葡萄酒的老大，但 Don 并不敢掉以轻心。守住这第一把交椅在瞬息万变的中国本来就不是件易事。更何况，他还有个更大的梦想，要把 ASC 打造成全球前十名的葡萄酒公司。前方不知道还有多少场暴风雨等待着他，但别忘了，Don 是头凶猛的豹子。

"I am a good entrepreneur stimulated by interaction with other people but not a good professional manager handling structure and systems," St Pierre Jr explains.

He now lives in Shanghai with his wife Monica Xu and daughters Caitlyn, Ciana and Callie.

He spends most of his time helping Japanese partner Suntory, which acquired a 70-percent share of ASC in 2009, to take advantage of global wine opportunities.

His aim is to build ASC into one of the world's top 10 wine companies.

1. 桃乐丝中国

公司由西班牙米高桃乐丝集团于1997年创立。2007年，法国罗思柴尔德男爵集团注资成为其重要股东之一。目前，已在中国七大主要城市设立了分公司和办事处，产品来自14个国家涵盖超过400个品种。

2. 由西往东美酒公司

公司成立于2003年，总部位于上海，现从10个国家进口400个不同种类葡萄酒。2012年，公司被中国侍酒师大赛授予"最佳进口商"称号。

3. 美夏国际贸易

公司成立于1999年，有两个创始人：美国人Ian Ford，原服务于全球葡萄酒与烈酒销售巨头Seagram；新西兰人Brendan O'Toole，原服务于波士顿咨询集团。目前公司在大中华地区进家代理60余家酒庄的葡萄酒，涵盖全球12个产酒国。公司名字美夏的出处很有意思。那年夏天，两位创始人在厦门顶的酒吧里一拍即合，决定在中国创业。公司名字就是为了纪念那个美丽的夏天。

4. 建发酒业

公司隶属于中国国有投资集团建发股份。1998年成立于福建省厦门市。2006年与欧洲最大的葡萄酒集团之一——CASTEL达成协议，成为其核心品牌Roche Mazet中国总代理。2007年起逐步扩张，代理产品遍步法国、美国、加拿大、德国、意大利、智利六国的葡萄酒。2009年，成为13家法国列级庄的中国总代理，并逐年增加。2011年，公司以1200万瓶的海关年进口量，成为中国最大的葡萄酒进口商之一。

中国具影响力精品葡萄酒经销商

181/197

中国
第一侍酒师的
杯酒人生

"我就像一杯产自德国莫塞尔的雷司令，清透、纯净。讨喜的甜美伴随着尖锐的酸度。这酒喝上去虽然含蓄内敛，但那份质感却是扎扎实实地存在。"中国第一侍酒师吕杨这样评价自己。

LU Yang is China's most decorated sommelier and he uses his Canadian training to promote wine as a "down-to-earth agricultural product that deserves to be enjoyed and appreciated by everyone." He talks to Ruby Gao.

Sommelier Lu Yang compares himself to a German Mosel Rieseling, "clean and pure with both light sweetness and sharp acidity, both implicit and substantive."

Wisdom of China's young wine sage

The 31-year-old wine steward also describes himself as "hard-working, goal-oriented, fortunate and overrated."

Lu is the top sommelier in China, one of Asia's best.

吕杨出生在新疆的克拉玛依，那里有触手可及的蓝天白云，一望无际的沙漠。自打他出生之日起，他就知道要人前笑，这一份控制情绪的天赋，好像生来就是要投身服务业的。这是一种讨喜的甜美，亲切而温暖，暖得像家乡的太阳。

2009 年，在奢华的上海半岛酒店，人们看到了这张笑容，他成了上海最受欢迎的侍酒师。人们喜欢去这家坐落于外滩的酒店，那里能听到诉说这座城市历史的钟声，看到对面陆家嘴美丽的天际线，当然，还有让人垂涎的美食美酒。

在位于酒店 13 层的 Sir Elly's 西餐厅，吕杨忙着和客人打招呼，穿梭于餐桌、后厨和酒窖之间。对用餐客人来说，如果厨师创造了味道，那么侍酒师就是用酒的语言和食物深层对话，编织想象的人。他被认作是一部学贯古今的葡萄酒活字典和鉴赏家，用他的专业为客人推荐葡萄酒，并提供配餐建议——一个优秀的侍酒师足以让客人的一餐从口腹的饱足升华到内心的感动。

"不好意思哦，我不太懂酒。"一个客人有点尴尬地合上了酒单。"这算什么问题，我请你喝杯尝尝看。"吕杨笑着拿出三个酒杯，根据客人点的食物，倒入了三种葡萄酒。酒让客人放松了些。吕杨试着和对方闲聊，从客人的神态表情中迅速判断出他们的喜好。

吕杨觉得与其说是酒配餐，不如说是酒配人。以四川菜为例，几乎全球最具分量的酒评家，包括 Robert Parker 和 Jancis Robinson，都觉得应该搭配较甜、酒体轻盈的雷司令来缓解菜的辣。可很多中国人好的就是那口辣，为什么不能用高酒精度的 Syrah 或是 Zinfandel 来让菜肴吃上去更辣呢？餐酒搭配大可随和些、灵活点，遵守大原则就好。若是太刻意，反而丧失了不少乐趣。

"我努力地向客人传递自己的理念'葡萄酒，没什么大不了'。的确，是有那么些酒，稀有、昂贵，甚至可以说是神圣到撼动人心。但多数情况下，他就是一个适合大家享受的农产品，何必要把它塑造成精英文化，搞得像爱马仕包那样不可亲近。当然，适当地引导客人也是需要的，品酒，就像是看一幅达芬奇的抽象画，如果没人在旁边告诉你作者想表达什么，你很难读懂它的美。"吕杨说起自己的品酒经来旁征博引，滔滔不绝。

难怪，半岛的客人里超过半数是不太懂酒的中国人，但这丝毫没有影响这位明星侍酒师轻易地卖完酒单上的酒。吕杨的老同事、半岛行政总厨 Terrance Crandall 说："吕杨就像是一座语言和文化的桥梁，将西方的葡萄酒文化和中国人连接到了一起。"

客人是那么喜欢他，可就在 2012 年下半年，他提交了辞呈，突然消失在众人的视线中。

A sommelier is romantically described as a person weaving a spell of imagination and constructing a deep dialogue with wine and food. Basically, he's deeply knowledgeable about wine and pairing it with food.

But Lu doesn't agree completely.

"Being a sommelier is actually about pairing wine with a person," Lu told Shanghai Daily in a recent interview in Hong Kong, where he is wine director at Shangri-La International Hotel Management. He is the first mainland Chinese to hold the position. Previously he was chief sommelier at The Peninsula Shanghai for three years, leaving in July.

Lu cites the classic example of many Western wine experts, including Robert Parker, who pair sweet white wine with Sichuan cuisine to balance its heat and spice. But Sichuanese and other Chinese diners appreciate the spicy, hot taste and choose strong, distilled grain liquor baijiu to fan the flames.

"For customers who love spicy food, why not pair Sichuan food with Zinfandel or Syrah, high in alcohol, to make the food taste more spicy?" Lu asks.

在伦敦拿下高级侍酒师的绿色勋章，吕杨把自己取得的成绩归因于中国葡萄酒市场的崛起。经济的腾飞缔造了大批拥有强大购买力、崇尚享受生活的人群。

此时的吕杨身处伦敦，心情如英格兰的天气般阴晴不定。他刚在那儿完成 Advanced Sommelier（高级侍酒师）的考试，又是论文，又是盲品，倍受煎熬。经过漫长的不安和等待，他终于拿到了那枚象征荣誉的绿色勋章，成了世界上第一个中国籍的高级侍酒师。全球范围内，拥有这枚勋章的，也就 500 多个人。在泰晤士河畔，这个 31 岁的年轻人认定了他的下一个目标，拿下那枚红色的勋章，代表着该领域至高无上的荣誉——Master Sommelier（侍酒师大师）。

消息传到中国，葡萄酒业内掌声一片，无不为他感到骄傲。也有人表示不屑，说道："葡萄酒是拿来喝的，又不是用来考的。Robert Parker 一个证也没考过，也不影响他成为全球最具影响力的酒评家。"

吕杨反驳，在今日这个浮躁的社会，自吹自擂横行，也就剩下证书可以客观地说明一些问题，证明一点能力。

"Wine pairing can be more flexible as long as larger principles are observed. If you analyze too much, you can lose plenty of direct pleasure," he says.

Prestigious honor

Lu has a varied biography: Born in the Xinjiang Uygur Autonomous Region, he returned to Shanghai, his father's hometown, for middle school, then moved to Canada to study physics in Toronto. He switched to viticulture.

Lu recently passed the Advanced Sommelier (AS) examination in England, organized by the Court of Master Sommeliers (CMS), the most authoritative examiner of credentials. He was the first Chinese and the second Asian to pass the exam. Only around 500 sommeliers can write AS after their name.

He's just one step away from Master Sommelier (MS), one of the highest accreditations, and plans to take the exam next year. The other top accreditation is Master of Wine, but Lu isn't rushing.

法国、美国、澳洲、新西兰、意大利，大凡是产酒的国家，无不视中国为金矿，挤破头想在这个市场分得一杯羹。酒商、庄主向餐厅和酒店大献殷勤，巴望着像吕杨这样的人能为他们背书。这使得中国的侍酒师们幸运地接触到了品类繁多的葡萄酒，大到波尔多、勃艮第名庄，小到那些不知名却极有趣的精品酒庄。

葡萄酒的世界里，喝过，才有权说话。

He acknowledges that some wine insiders consider the AS certificate useless, saying wine is for drinking, not exams, noting that masters such as Robert Parker don't hold any certificate.

But still Lu believes that "certificates are one of the few things available in a fast-paced era filled with self-promoters to prove my abilities objectively."

He attributes his success largely to the emerging Chinese wine market.

Global vintners and distributors see China as a vast and growing market with irresistible potential, rushing to sell their wines in China. They need knowledgeable sommeliers to help them win Chinese customers.

"We, Chinese sommeliers, have access to diverse wine, from big-name chateaux to some unknown interesting wines," Lu says.

In a new and immature market with few knowledgeable consumers, many people unquestioningly admire Chinese wine experts, including sommeliers, critics, writers and educators.

"There's a gap between the reputation of these experts, including me, and their level of expertise. I am overrated," Lu says.

Though he's planning to take the MS exam, right now he's adapting to his new job.

2012 年 12 月，吕杨在香港，身份是香格里拉酒店集团的全球葡萄酒总监，成了第一个坐上这个职位的大陆人。亚洲第一葡萄酒收藏家唐英年说："哦，吕杨，我知道，就是那个大陆来的侍酒师！"

新出炉的高级侍酒师并没有从伦敦回到上海。在位于港岛英皇道的香格里拉总部，吕总监正忙着编写集团的侍酒师守则。厚厚的一本，制定了集团的葡萄酒发展宏图和策略，事无巨细地规范了酒店的侍酒流程和服务标准。

"我希望他的加入，能让香格里拉的客人，无论是在巴黎还是山东青岛，都能享受到同等专业细致的服务。没有人比他更适合这个职位。集团有一半的酒店在中国，他知道如何和一线员工沟通。而他自身的明星光环也有助于香格里拉聚拢中国最顶尖的葡萄酒人才。无论是在一线还是二线城市，葡萄酒新人们视他为中国梦的代表，他们总是说，如果吕杨可以，为什么我不行？"他的老板，香格里拉集团餐饮总监 Jean Marc Dizerens 说道。

New journey

Lu made a name for himself over three years as chief sommelier at The Peninsula Shanghai. When he left the hotel in July, insiders were watching for his next stage in his career.

They found out soon enough. Lu is now writing a sommelier's manual and establishing Shangri-La Group's vision, strategy and wine standards. It will be published within the hotel group next month.

The manual or Sommeliers' Guide will ensure the wine experience in Shangri-La Paris and Shangri-La Qingdao are at the same level, says Jean Marc Dizerens, director of corporate food and beverage (operations).

"He perfectly fits the position. To enhance the wine image of the hotel group, with half of its hotels in China, Yang not only has solid wine knowledge but also knows how to communicate with our Asian staff," Dizerens says.

It doesn't hurt that Lu is a star.

吕杨在香港的成名源于一年前在 Wine Future 高峰论坛上的一场名为"寻找葡萄酒的中国口味"的主题演讲。会场的讲台上，闪烁着当今业内最夺目的光芒，Robert Parker、Jancis Robinson。向来淡定的他在台上有些紧张。

在演讲中，吕杨提到，根本没有所谓的中国口味。中国人需要的不是取悦和迎合，而是西方世界能给予真正意义上的尊重和耐心。他所指的"中国口味"是指大批西方酿酒师们绞尽脑汁想酿造符合中国人喜好的葡萄酒。在他们看来，中国人的口味是奇怪的。

"我们的味蕾和西方人没有差别。世界是平的，大家，尤其我们年轻的一代都是吃着汉堡包喝着可乐长大的。我们的口味发展，遵循着美国、澳洲等新世界国家的发展规律，从偏爱简单的果香与甜味慢慢走向寻求更多的复杂和平衡。"

"Whether you go to a first- or second-tier city in China, people see him as an inspiration and a model of a Chinese achieving his dream. Many Chinese in the wine industry ask themselves 'If Yang can do it, why can't I'," says Dizerens, who has worked in China for 10 years and is familiar with the effect of star power in motivating people.

Lu's celebrity started at his previous position in Shanghai - he even gave more interviews than senior hotel management.

"Yang is a bridge linking Western wine culture with Chinese, not just linguistically but also culturally," says Terrence Crandall, an executive chef and a former colleague of Lu's.

In the past few years, Lu has promoted wine culture by teaching classes. He also translated the "How To Taste Wine" (2011) by Jancis Robinson from English into Chinese. The popular book is used in many wine appreciation classes.

演讲结束，台下掌声如雷。

吕杨坦言，自己的观点，和在上海
世博会期间经历的一次不愉快的葡
萄酒晚宴有关。当晚，波尔多名庄
的代表几乎全到齐了，各个身着正
装以示尊重。酒过三巡，一个法国
人醉醺醺地走到吕杨面前，傲慢略
带嘲讽地说："多亏你们中国人在
2008 年全球金融危机的时候买下了
我们最差最便宜的酒，不然我们早
活不下去了。"

岁月悄然地打磨着这个年轻人的棱
角。内心再有不甘，他收起了锋芒，
选择了沉默。

他曾一度想考出 Master of Wine（葡
萄酒大师）和 Master Sommelier（侍
酒师大师）。这是葡萄酒专业人士
的终极梦想。全世界同时拥有这两
个头衔的才 4 个人。但现在，他暂
时停止了 Master of Wine 的冲刺。

现在的他，已然没有了自己的生活。
出个门、吃个饭都会带上小册子随
时随地做品酒笔记。工作外的假期
全用于出国参观葡萄酒产区和酒
庄。剩下来的那一点点时间，是用
来进行案头工作和理论学习的。

Communicator

When Lu worked as a sommelier at the Shanghai five-star hotel on the Bund, Chinese represented half of his customers and many know little about wine. But Lu sold out many wines on his list and developed his own approach to explaining and serving wine to Chinese customers.

"My wine philosophy transmitted to the customer is 'Don't see wine as too serious.' Although there are some expensive, even sacred wines that can touch your heart, under most circumstances wine should not be an indicator of elite group like an Hermes bag, but purely a down-to-earth agricultural product that deserves enjoyed and appreciated by everyone," Lu says.

When diners say they know nothing and are mystified by the wine list, Lu always smiles and says, "That's not a problem." He then serves several different samples, depending on what they plan to order.

"After customers drink the wine, which relaxes them, I chat casually, read them quickly and recommend the right wine," the sommelier says.

他曾看不惯中国葡萄酒圈子里存在的那些华而不实，利欲熏心，对那些半桶水使劲晃悠的假专家更是嗤之以鼻。在中国这样一个新兴的缺乏历史与传统的葡萄酒市场，懂酒的极少。于是大众对那些鱼目混珠的侍酒师，葡萄酒作家、教育家趋之若鹜，盲目追捧。吕杨甚至一度认为自己的专业水平也是被高估的。可现在，他的想法改变了：十年之后，再回过头去看那些南郭先生，他们对中国葡萄酒的发展仍然有值得肯定之处。客观上，他们鼓动了大批人进入葡萄酒的世界。

He also subtly guides returning wine beginners.

Lu compares wine to abstract painting. At first, many people get nothing from it, unless someone helps them appreciate it.

"That's not cheating but a way of guiding people to better enjoy wine," Lu says.

The Chinese edition of "How to Taste Wine" translated by Lu is the most popular book in Chinese Amazon's wine category.

"The small book ends my confusion about wine. There's no flowery language, no pretentious showing off wine knowledge, but simply sharing master-level expertise. Real thanks to Robinson and Lu Yang," wrote reader Chen Tao on the Amazon website.

"Lu is a talented translator. Youth gives his translation a lively character. His professionalism standardizes Chinese wine vocabulary (referring to grape varieties and production areas)," says Qiu Hong, senior editor of the publisher, Shanghai Sanlian Bookstore.

Initially Lu translated the book out of personal interest because it inspired him during his wine studies. But it was hard work and Lu calls it his first and last translation.

"I would rather die than translate again. Jancis' British English with subordinate clauses is a huge challenge," Lu explains.

Lu is also a certified wine educator in China, teaching WSET (Wine and Spirit Education Trust) courses to nurture wine professionals.

旧照上的吕杨顶着一头摇滚青年范儿的长发，懒懒地坐在一堆零乱的酒桶前面，和眼前西装革履的他天差地别。吕杨说，那张照片是在加拿大的 Le Clos Jordanne 酒庄工作时照的，那个酒庄离尼亚加拉大瀑布很近。

---

12 岁那年，他跟随着身为援疆知青的父亲回到了上海。读初中的时候，他最强的科目是地理，这为他日后研究全球的葡萄酒产区及风土打下了扎实的基础。到了 19 岁，吕杨和很多上海学生一样选择了出国留学，入读多伦多大学物理系。头两年，他成绩优异，全 A 通过。但到了第三年，他开始迷茫，渐渐颓废到成天沉湎于酒精，无所事事。直到有一天，他偶然间来到了尼亚加拉大瀑布旁的一片葡萄园里，葡萄树一字排开，有个声音在他心里回荡：这才是你吕杨应该做的事情。

顶着父母的强烈反对，他选择了退学，并转入尼亚加拉学院攻读葡萄酒种植和酿造。那是他人生最辛苦的两年，父母对他失望透顶，断了经济资助，他只能半工半读。班上的同学多数是持有侍酒师资质来进一步深造的，他却对葡萄酒一无所知。同学们在品酒课上闻到了桃子、烟草、蜂蜜和菌菇的香气，吕杨觉得人家根本就是在瞎扯。

"He's humble and flexible and doesn't follow all the old rules. His blackboard writing with numerous arrows and his focus on practical wine-tasting impresses me," says Jeuce Huang, managing director of Taste. ly Communication and one of Lu's students.

"I am not a professional teacher but a kind one. I care about my student a lot," Lu says,

His efforts to promote wine culture in China won him an invitation to address Wine Future Hong Kong 2011, the year's premiere even in the global wine industry. He was one of only mainland speakers and he discussed "The Chinese Wine Palate."

"I never thought one day I would stand beside Robert Parker and Jancis Robinson," the young sommelier says. "I mainly argued for giving the Chinese market more respect and showing patience."

毕业之后，他考出了注册侍酒师，在 Le Clos Jordanne 找到了一份助理酿酒师的工作。在酒庄里，他发现了书本上所没有的关于葡萄酒的奥秘和乐趣。他的第二份工作是在多伦多高级餐厅 Canoe 担任助理侍酒师，那是他第一次了解什么是国际标准的侍酒服务，也是头一回尝试着去管理一间大型酒窖。

餐厅的工作固然繁忙，他却用业余时间将 Jancis Robinson 的品酒练习册翻译成了中文。这本译作自推出以来就稳居亚马逊葡萄酒类书籍的畅销榜首位。这是吕杨的第一本也是最后一本译作。他说，太累，太辛苦，打死也不干了。

如今的吕杨，不再一味地追求完美，而选择活在当下。希望有机会还能做回当年的那个开着哈雷机车的少年。

Chinese wine consumers should be treated the same as Westerners, however, winemakers from both the New World and Old World now try to make wine especially to appeal to the "Chinese palate," Lu tells Shanghai Daily.

"The so-called Chinese palate doesn't exist. The world is flat. Chinese, especially the younger generation, grow up with Coca-Cola and hamburgers. We have the same wine palate as Westerners, starting out preferring fruity wine with a sweet touch and gradually turning to wine with complexity," Lu says.

He resents Western wine snobs who dismiss China's developing taste. At the 2010 Shanghai World Expo, Lu dined with representatives of a famous Bordeaux chateau.

"After a Frenchman got drunk, he told me contemptuously, 'In 2008, when the world financial crises crushed the two big wine markets in the UK and the US, it was the Chinese who kept us alive by buying plenty of our cheap wine'," he recalls.

Desert beginnings

Karamay in northern Xinjiang is where Lu started out and got a feel for nature.

"I was born to the hospitality industry since I am always smiling," he says, recalling that no matter how sad he was, he would always smile for a camera.

"Sometimes, especially when I am working, smiles are like bandages covering up my pain," Lu says.

He calls Karamay "a place where the blue sky is close at hand, the horizon is distant and the Gobi Desert is underfoot. It's the most beautiful memory of my life."

When he was 12 years old, Lu moved to Shanghai, since his father is Shanghainese. In middle school, his favorite subject was geography, which contributed to his interest in wine terroir and production areas.

When he was 19, he went to Toronto, Canada, to study physics at the University of Toronto.

After two years, he found himself drawn to alcohol and idleness, in his own words. He dropped out but had always been drawn to local vineyards.

"Grape vines told me that wine was what I would do seriously," he says.

He studied viticulture at Niagara College, calling those two years the hardest in his life since he knew nothing about wine while many classmates already were sommeliers.

"When they talked about notes of peach, mushroom, tobacco and honey in wine, I thought that was total bullshit," Yang says.

His parents were upset when he quit physics since they wanted him to become a respected professor. That meant he had to finance his own wine studies.

He graduated with a sommelier's certification from the International Sommelier Guild and became a winemaker's assistant at Le Clos Jordanne, a winery in Niagara. Eight months there gave him invaluable information not found in books.

He then became a sommelier's assistant at Canoe, a fine dining restaurant in Toronto, where he learned about wine serving and managing a cellar.

In 2010, when he was 29, Lu returned to Shanghai and became a sommelier.

Today in Hong Kong, he says, "I have no life but work with wine." When he dines out with his friends, he takes notes on the wines.

He spends his holidays visiting wine production areas. He studies and teaches.

"I need some space of my own," Lu admits. "Marinating in wine all day long creates some aesthetic fatigue."

He says it's time to take up a very different hobby, riding big motorcycles. His dream is to own a Harley-Davidson.

'Fake experts'

Lu remains dedicated to the Chinese wine industry, but describes some of it as "frivolous, profit-driven, and filled with dilettantes marketing themselves as experts."

Once he was furious with those "experts," but he's mellowed, saying. "When we look back in 10 years, we'll see the benefits of 'fake experts' outweigh the damage, since they attract people and stimulate curiosity."

One day he plans to make his own wine, saying "the vineyard is a place that's pure and simple."

His dream is to open his own wine bar in Shanghai, where he can promote his wine philosophy. He's waiting for the right time and place.

"It will be funky and natural, probably decorated with swings and my favorite paintings," he says. The wines will high-quality boutique drops "with affordable prices so more people can really enjoy the beauty of wine."

Rachel Wang
Independent wine journalist

"Lu Yang's talented, smart and humble, like a balanced and fine old wine. There're few people who don't like him."

Jerry Liao
Chief sommelier at Jing'an Shangri-La, West Shanghai

"He's like a bottle of Burgundy Pinot Noir, easy to approach for beginners while profound for wine professionals. The more you get to know him, the more elegance and positive energy you harvest."

1. 郭莹

上海浦东四季酒店首席侍酒师，曾就职于米其林三星大厨 Jean Georges 在上海外滩三号开的同名法餐厅。她于 2015 年初在伦敦通过了 Advanced Sommelier（高级侍酒师）考试，成为中国第一批获得此资质的女性侍酒师。同时，她也是 2012 年中国最佳侍酒师的冠军。2013 年来获华盛顿世界青年侍酒师大赛第四名。（ps. 美女一名）

2. 廖唯一

上海静安香格里拉首席侍酒师，中国最早投身侍酒行业的元老之一。

3. 赵怀强

上海文华东方首席侍酒师。2014 年获得中国侍酒师大赛冠军及最佳侍酒服务奖。

4. 李美玉

北京柏悦酒店葡萄酒总监，曾受训于伦敦米其林二星餐厅 Le Gavroche。2011 年获得中国侍酒师大赛冠军。

中国优雅侍酒师

201 / 229

王不见王——
改写亚洲葡萄酒历史的
两个女人

Debra 和李志延，两人是同期 2008 年考出的葡萄酒大师，又都常驻香港。媒体习惯称 Debra 是亚洲第一位葡萄酒大师，李志延是全球第一位亚裔葡萄酒大师。更重要的是，两人都是女人，且都是漂亮的女人。她们成为葡萄酒大师，从某种意义上，改写了亚洲葡萄酒的历史，意味着女性拥有了至高无上的话语权。

2 female
wine experts
liken themselves
to Pinot Noir

当我要写一篇关于 Debra 和李志延的文章时，葡萄酒圈内很多人都认为我疯了。她们两人之间到底存着怎样的微妙关系不得而知，但互不同台却是个客观的事实。

翻看她们的过去，或多或少露出些许端倪。

一直到 Jancis Robinson 出现之前，当代葡萄酒向来是被男性垄断的天下，更不用说是男权主义牢牢扎根的亚洲。从男女生理特征来看，这样的状态并不合理。大量的研究发现，就葡萄酒鉴赏所依赖的嗅觉和味觉两方面，女性远比男性敏锐，更能分辨出细腻的差别。行业社交方面，女性也拥有无法企及的特权。在欧美的葡萄酒晚宴上，女性永远被安排坐在最重要的男性身边，比如庄主、酿酒师，或是酒商总经理。在中国，这等重要礼仪似乎被贯彻得不够彻底，不然的话，我这本书一定更厚。

全世界范围内目前拥有 304 个葡萄酒大师 (这个数字到本书出版之日可能有变化)，其中 90 位是女性。据说，这也是世界上通过率最低的考试。从 1990 年到 2000 年，有 266 个人参加考试，成功的才 85 人。

遗憾的是中国现在还没有属于自己的葡萄酒大师。大陆地区强有力的竞争者包括本书采访过的李晨光、吕杨，还有葡萄酒讲师施晔、郝利文。他们多数都皱着眉头，表示这是一个艰难到有些残酷的梦想。若非辞掉本职工作全身心投入，真的很难成功。有人每天五点起床，练习写 3 个小时的论文，九点上班，这样坚持 5 年，还是失败了。有人为此付出了 10 年，最终无法承受大师之重。

不论 Debra 和李志延本人是否承认这点帮助了她们成功，她们都有个有钱的老公。钱在葡萄酒的世界里意味着时间、精力、视野和味蕾。不用为五斗米折腰，只读圣贤书，需要的时候飞到波尔多、勃艮第、托斯卡纳，来一次说走就走的旅行，研究当地的风土，品尝对于很多人来说可能一辈子都无法承受的名庄酒，这是获得这个头衔必要的奢侈。

如果条件允许，真应该去比较下这两位大师完全不同的演讲风格和个人魅力。Jeannie(李志延)静如处子，严肃内敛，如学者般严谨地阐述葡萄酒里的科学，并创造了属于亚洲人自己的葡萄酒语言；Debra 动如脱兔，热情奔放，用寓教于乐的形式做了大量的葡萄酒文化普及，她更像是个能和粉丝打成一片的娱乐明星，时不时脱口而出：嘿！那穿着夏威夷草裙的男人像不像长相思葡萄酒？我家那只猫叫 Musigny（勃艮第一村庄）！

两人共同的导师 Patrick Farrell 说道，虽然她们性格不同，但有共同点：聪明，勤奋，专注，有悟性，更重要的是对梦想很执着。

更有意思的是两人都把自己比作是一杯来自勃艮第的黑品诺。葡萄酒的美不就在于它的仁者见仁和不可预知吗？即使同为勃艮第黑品诺，也拥有李志延和 Debra 两种截然不同的味道。

亲爱的读者们，如果你身边正好有一瓶勃艮第红酒，不如现在就把它打开，跟随着我的文字，去慢慢品味两位大师的成长故事。

女神李志延把自己比作是一杯来自勃艮第的黑品诺，一开始让人觉得轻柔，轻柔到让人费解，但柔软的背后却藏着一股难以撼动的力量，那是一份对理想和信念的坚定和忠诚。

女神总不是那么接地气，更何况她是李志延，全球第一个长着东方面孔的葡萄酒大师。李志延的故事全藏在她那双眼睛里，明亮，坚毅，充满智慧的灵动，似乎每一秒都在思考，却又透出一种令人难以琢磨的距离感。

女神有多美？今年 46 岁的她曾和跳水皇后郭晶晶一起为雅诗兰黛的眼霜代言。但不是所有的人都喜欢她，说得再不客气些，很多人都不怎么喜欢她，尤其是她的性格，觉得她有些"sophisticated and serious（复杂，世故且严肃）"。这或许要从她的童年说起。

李志延是美籍韩裔，出生在首尔，在很小的时候就随着父母移民美国。她的成长和多数活跃于西方社会的亚裔精英很像。没有根基，也没有显赫的家室，那就只能靠着努力读书奋斗出一片天来。终于，她考进了哈佛。一日哈佛，终生不同，这是许多美国新移民对常春藤的迷信。

Master of Wine (MW), a coveted qualification issued by The Institute of Masters of Wine in the United Kingdom, is the holy grail for some wine professionals. It's the highest title in the wine world, along with equally prestigious Master Sommelier (MS). Both are notoriously difficult to obtain.

Only 304 people from 24 countries and regions today can write MW after their names, and 90 of them are women, according to the institute. The exam is punishing and the passing rate is extremely low: Often one or two a year make the grade. From 1993 to 2000, only 85 of 266 candidates passed the exam.

"It's hard because the institute's mission and vision is striving for excellence in wine education," says Lynne Sherriff, chairman of the institute from 2010 to 2012. She was in town last Friday to chair the China Wine Challenge hosted by Hilton Shanghai.

"Single-minded, determined and focused make a MW," Sherriff says.

葡萄酒对于她的童年、青少年来说都是个遥远而模糊的影子，直到有一天，她作为交换生在英国牛津大学待了一年。牛津让人着迷的，除了那些古老而伟岸的巴洛克建筑，还有藏匿于其地下的巨大酒窖。酒窖有多老，这里面的酒就有多少岁。牛津的教授有一个特别的福利，可以以较低的价格购入那些昂贵的葡萄酒。于是，能参加教授举办的葡萄酒晚宴成为了牛津学子最大的期待之一。

那天晚上，李志延清楚地记得，那是她平生第一次接触那些所谓的绝世佳酿。

"我当时被震撼了。一款酒竟然可以有那么多充满层次的味道，这种感觉就像是为这本来平淡到寡味的英国菜注入了迷人的香料，瞬间鲜活起来。"她回忆道。

后面的故事不用说也能猜到，葡萄酒从此成为了她的挚爱。但长期以来，葡萄酒都是欧洲人的天下。通过奋斗改变命运在这块讲求历史和血统的大陆似乎不怎么行得通。

There is no Chinese MW so far, but 10 Chinese candidates are now preparing for the exam, including Huang Shan, a leading wine writer based in Beijing, and Fongyee Walker, director of Beijing-based Dragon Phoenix Wine Consultants. Among the 10, two are from China's mainland, with the other eight from Hong Kong.

"I believe there will be more Chinese involved but the process is steady and slow. China wasn't open to the West until very recent and language is also a barrier," says Sherriff.

This week, Shanghai Daily interviewed two female MWs, both actively involved in Chinese wine education: Korean Jeannie Cho Lee, the first Asian MW, and American Debra Meiburg, the first MW in Asia.

Both are based in Hong Kong and received their MW in 2008, and both are active in the China market.

"他们觉得我来自一个没有葡萄酒传统的家庭，抑或说，没有葡萄酒历史的国度，根本就没有资格评判他们的酒，尤其是那些充满历史的老酒。"李志延说。

成为葡萄酒大师是对自己，也是对这些欧洲人最好的证明。

考取葡萄酒大师是一场马拉松式的角逐，对于已为人妻为人母的李志延来说，困难是加倍的。她感叹，最难的大概是2003年，那时她和投身金融业的老公已定居在香港，四个孩子们都还小，最大的不到六岁。女神的每一天都是在品酒，写论文，查资料交杂着换尿布，做饭和孩子们的哭天抢地中度过的。2005年，她在考试中失败了。

"毅然决然的心和丈夫的支持是我最大的动力。我曾告诉自己，你可以输但不能放弃，放弃意味你根本就没有尽全力。"李志延说道。

3年后，她成功了。

"They share a good number of characteristics: very intelligent, diligent, easy to instruct, focused and goal-oriented. They also brought a business and management strategy for success to the MW program, and then to the world of wine after they passed," says Patrick Farrell, their common mentor, also a MW. Farrell is CEO and president of Inventive Technologies, Inc/BevWizard Co.

Asked how they would describe themselves as a wine, the two female MWs both describe themselves as a glass of Pinot Noir, but interpret it in very different ways.

Meiburg is outgoing, teaching wine in a lively, often funny and memorable way. A writer, she also calls herself a wine "edu-tainer."

Another writer, Lee is very academic, devising a new wine terminology for aromas and flavors involving Asian ingredients that are familiar to new Asian wine tasters.

"Their potential in China is unlimited. They have the knowledge of both wine and the culture to bridge gaps that others may not able to accomplish," says Farrell.

直到现在，她依然保持着当年那种高强度的工作习惯。采访她的那天，已是下午四点，虽然女神的脸上透出一点点倦意，但丝毫没有影响她拍照时摆出专业的姿势，回答问题时思维敏捷，说话严谨。若不是采访完吃饭的时候，她没等甜品上来，就抱歉地提前告退，很难想象那天她是早上四点起床，赶最早的班机从香港到上海，又马不停蹄地讲课，品酒，中间没有停歇过。

生活中，我们孜孜不倦在追求的，往往是自己不曾拥有的那块空白。虽然不知道李志延努力的动力是什么，但从表面的人生轨迹看，她一直想往高处爬。她的言语中，也不乏对"上面"那个位置的捍卫。

"葡萄酒的确可以给你的人生带来快乐，但生活中有太多东西远比它重要。你应该把它看成是一种奢侈品，那是一种坐拥家庭、财富和健康之后才去追逐的东西。"她在采访中当被问及个人的葡萄酒哲学时说道。

女神觉得自己是个严谨的学者，根本无力招架那些通过电视学习葡萄酒的观众："他们排斥复杂，总想着要我给出一个简单、直白而快速的答案。这让我非常的不自在。"

A Chinese wine insider, who declines to be identified, downplays their significance.

"They charge very high prices to hold commercial wine seminars to get a piece of pie in the growing Chinese wine market because they are MWs. But their real contribution here is limited," says the wine insider.

Academic: Asians need own wine lingo

Jeannie Cho Lee, the first ethnic Asian master of wine, describes herself as a Burgundy Pinot Noir, "initially not very easy to understand and seeming kind of light and soft, but with strength, fundamental values and integrity behind that softness."

Lee was the first wine expert to systematically describe wine using terms more understandable to Asians, such as dried mushroom, jujube and star anise.

Born in Seoul, Lee moved to the United States at an early age and studied at Harvard. Since 1994 she has been living in Hong Kong where she is a leading wine writer, critic and educator and mother of four daughters.

李志延的一个拥趸说："我无法判断她的形容对与不对。但最起码，这给了我一定的自信与勇气去接触葡萄酒。这辈子都没吃过黑加仑，你让我怎么从红酒中闻到它的味道。"

李志延主要活跃在香港，她在大陆地区的影响力得益于两本被翻译成中文的著作《东品西酿》和《东膳西酿》。两本书里，她史无前例地创造了属于亚洲人自己的品酒语言及餐酒搭配系统，尽管这些在全球范围内饱受争议。

即使成为了葡萄酒大师，也无法改变欧美人对亚洲面孔的偏见。这让李志延萌发了一种强烈的意愿：用亚洲人自己的方式去思考葡萄酒，去传达一种真正意义上的文化自信。这份独立与自主才能帮助亚洲人融入葡萄酒的世界，而非游走在边缘。

The 45-year-old wine master is known in China for two prize-winning books, "Asian Palate" (2009), the first book systematically pairing wine with Asian food, and "Mastering Wine for the Asian Palate" (2011), which gave prominence to Asia's own wine vocabulary. Both are written in English and translated into Chinese.

Lee says she's more like a scholar, serious and rigorous.

"I try to make wine easy to understand without making it too simple," she said in Shanghai last month in an interview with Shanghai Daily.

Besides wine, Lee has a passion for food, which inspired her first book. She holds a Certificat de Cuisine from Le Cordon Bleu. She's also a Master Sake Sommelier, awarded by Japan's Sake Service Institute.

It's much harder for a young-looking Asian woman to be a recognized wine master, says Lee, adding that there's a lot of pressure. Some European vineyard owners have mistakenly thought she was not experienced enough to judge their wines.

"When they, especially Europeans, see me, their first impression is that I am not from a wine-making family. My history with wine is not so long, especially with fine old wines," says Lee.

Motherhood also took time away from wine study. In 2003, when she was seriously studying for her MW, she had four children under six years old. She attributes her success to her determination and her husband's support.

"I can fail but never quit. Quit means you didn't even try hard," says Lee.

在《东品西酿》中，她把那些西方的品酒词进行了本土化，开创了一门由亚洲食材主导的葡萄酒语言。举例来说，西方酒评家经常用雪松、黑加仑、薄荷、烟草来形容赤霞珠，她却用干菇、红枣、青椒和绿茶叶。西方喜欢用覆盆子、车厘子、紫罗兰来形容黑品诺的香气，她把这些"翻译"成杨梅、泰国茉莉和枸杞。白葡萄酒也一样，以芳香的赛美容为例，西方喜欢用柑橘、香草、杏子来描述，她则"翻译"成杨桃、竹笋、白芝麻和蟠桃，霞多丽里面的矿物味，她直接译成海带。

这样的创举将李志延推上了一个尴尬的位置。西方的主流声音认为，这些所谓的本土化根本就是牵强附会，哗众取宠；更有人认为这根本就是一种商业概念炒作。

但在中国，很多葡萄酒爱好者却为她拍手喝彩。

"或许欧洲人无法理解。但我的本意从来就没有想去取代现有的品酒词，只是希望让全球的葡萄酒语言更多元和全面。更何况，这些品酒词并非凭空捏造，而是基于我非常严谨的研究和分析。"李志延解释道。

Being a woman has its advantages. "In a lot of wine tastings and dinners, I usually sit next to the most important person because I am a woman," says Lee.

Broadening wine lexicon

Familiar terms such as cedar, plum, mint and tobacco are not the only words Lee uses to describe Cabernet Sauvignon. It can also be described with flavors familiar to Asians, such as dried mushroom, dried jujube, green pepper and green tea leaf. Raspberry, cherry and violets are traditionally used to describe Pinot Noir, but waxberry, medlar and Thai jasmine flower can also be used.

The fragrance of Semillon can be described as citrus, fresh herbs, preserved apricot, star fruit, bamboo shoot and white sesame.

Describing wine flavors in Asian terms for a fast-growing wine market sets Lee apart from many wine experts.

"Asians are becoming very important consumers and producers. We must expand our vocabulary to have our (Asian) perspectives," she says.

从蓝莓到红枣，从紫罗兰到泰国茉莉，这其中到底经历了怎样的过程？李志延从 600 种基本的亚洲食材开始，去寻找他们在葡萄酒中相对应的香气。渐渐地，她发现这其中有很多香气是高度相似的，比如松露和木鱼花、紫罗兰和茉莉花叶、荔枝和龙眼。但她也承认，并不是所有的香气都能本土化，比如酒评家们会用 brioche（一种奶油面包卷）来形容有年纪的香槟或是勃艮第白葡萄酒中特有的烘烤香气。她对于自己的这套品酒词充满信心，正联络 WSET，希望它们能纳入国际通行的考试用词。

她的另一本讨论亚洲餐配酒的《东膳西酿》可就没那么好运了。虽然，李志延谦虚地表示，餐酒搭配从来就没有标准答案，但书里牵涉到大量的中餐，很多中国人并不买账，觉得，李志延最多也就在韩国菜配酒上有发言权，但讨论中国菜似乎并不够格。

女神从来没有公开回应过这些非议，但曾经强调，自己在法国蓝带餐饮学院受过专业培训，对日本清酒的研究也颇有造诣，拿到了清酒大师侍酒师的从业资质。

"I have never tasted blackcurrant and raspberry in my life. How can I get these aromas from wine?" asks wine lover Faye Gu. "Many Shanghai wine classes still use classical Western wine vocabulary, which challenges entry-level wine lovers like me."

"Lee's vocabulary makes my tasting much easier," Gu adds.

Andrea Zhu, Lee's Chinese publisher, cites readers as saying that Asian terminology makes wine more accessible.

"Lee helps popularize wine culture here to reach more people," says Lu Yang, wine director at Shangri-La Group.

Lee's innovative, culture-specific terminology has its skeptics among wine experts, who say it lacks precision and is adaptation for adaptation's sake.

"Maybe the Europeans don't understand. But it's just the same as our (Asians) not knowing what a currant is. Asian ingredients are not supposed to replace the Western, I just expand the flavor descriptions to make them acceptable," Lee explains.

"我在这本书里并不是仅仅提供黑品诺配北京烤鸭的配餐建议，更多的是去分析食物背后的味觉结构，引导读者自己去寻找答案。"李志延说。

李志延为了写这本书，先后拜访了亚洲十大美食之都，包括上海、北京、香港、台北、首尔、新加坡、曼谷、吉隆坡和孟买。每个城市，她都停留了一个月去深入当地厨房，寻访当地名厨。书里，她对所有的食物进行酸、甜、苦、鲜、油、肥六方面的打分，再将其和葡萄酒中的单宁、酸度和酒体进行配对，从而寻求一种和谐。

客观来说，她这本书的一大贡献是填补了世界范围内对鲜这个味道的阐述和分析的空白。毕竟，这个味觉只存在于亚洲菜系里，连英文的翻译都是照搬日文"umami"。

她在书中写道，存在于食物里的鲜味自身就很细腻轻柔，并且会带出葡萄酒里那种又咸又苦又带有泥土气息的味道，因而在搭配的时候要格外的小心，尽量选取同样细致柔和丝滑的葡萄酒。

Comparing the aroma of dried jujube to that of blueberry and mint to green bell pepper is based on research and experience, she says. Lee began with 600 Asian ingredients and narrowed them down to suit particular wines and explain terms that otherwise might be inexplicable.

Lee sees similarities in the aromas of truffle and bonito (tuna) flakes, lychee and longan, violet and jasmine tea leaf, mineral content and wakame seaweed.

Not all Western wine terms can be adapted for Asian, Lee says. She cites "brioche" to describe the baked aroma of old Champagne and mature white Burgundy.

She is now talking to the Wine and Spirit Education Trust to rewrite their educational materials, incorporating the Asia-specific vocabulary she uses. "They (Westerners) can use theirs and we can use ours."

李志延透露，她正着手自己的第三本书，名字暂定为"The Growth and History of Fine Wine." 这次，她将目光对准了中国的高端精品酒市场，探讨其过去三十年来的演变和发展。她认为，未来拉菲、拉图这些名庄酒会在商务宴请中逐渐取代燕鲍翅和茅台的地位，毕竟人人都想表现自己的好品味。这也会带来连带效应，中国人谈生意的氛围和节奏会逐渐改变，从原先的干杯醉倒发展为一种更为平缓却又复杂的氛围。

采访的时候，中国的抵制三公消费大幕才刚刚揭开，葡萄酒高端市场所承受的影响和打击还未显现。不知道李志延时至今日是否仍坚持同样的解读和判断？

Lee says she is confident that her vocabulary will eventually become part of a universal wine language because more Asian ingredients are used by chefs worldwide.

No single answer

Before Lee wrote it, there was no guide on pairing wine with Asian food.

"Asian Palate" doesn't just make recommendations (Pinot Noir with Peking duck), but also explores how the components of flavor in food and wine react to and complement each other.

"There's no one simple answer in pairing because everyone's palate is different. I just analyze and encourage readers to find answers by themselves," says Lee.

For example, tannins in wine accentuate the spiciness in food, so why should spicy food lovers serve a less tannic wine?

Many people, especially a TV audience, want a simple, direct and quick answer, not a complicated one, she says. But "when I have to give a very simple answer, I'm very dissatisfied."

Lee has studied 10 Asian food cities, Shanghai, Beijing, Hong Kong, Taipei, Seoul, Tokyo, Singapore, Bangkok, Kuala Lumpur and Mumbai. In each city she spent a month in kitchens, talking with chefs and exploring and rating the importance of various flavors and ingredients - sweet, sour, bitter, umami, oil and fat. Each is ranked from 1 to 5.

开始讲白葡萄酒雷司令的时候，Debra 请了个魁梧的男同学上台，把那条蓬蓬裙套在了他身上。

"看，这就是雷司令的特征，香气温婉娇柔，但内在的骨架却是个十足刚毅的男人。"她拿起一杯酒边喝边说。

同样把自己比喻为黑品诺，亚洲第一位葡萄酒大师 Debra Meiburg 把自己比作是一杯来自勃艮第的黑品诺，调皮而灵动的果香里混合着一丝性感的挑逗，但骨子里却蕴含着一股强大到难以撼动的能量。

"你确定她用的单词是 flirty（挑逗）？怎么可能有女人愿意这样形容自己？"我的老外编辑一脸狐疑。

可 Debra 就是那么特别。她散发出的性感令男人着迷，又不让女人讨厌，还成功地挑逗了中国人的葡萄酒味蕾。她应该是这本书里最接地气的人物，上海近十万辆出租车上都曾循环播放她的葡萄酒教学视频"品尝葡萄酒"。

"我影响了所有的出租车司机！"Debra 大笑。

She then looks at the flavors and structure of wine, such as the tannins, acidity and body, and sees how the food and a wine react with each other.

"Before Lee, few people analyzed the relationship between umami flavor with wine," says publisher Zhu.

"Umami brings out earthy, bitter or savory notes in wine. It is both delicate and savory, thus, wines need equal delicacy and subtlety with emphasis on wine's silky tannin texture and mouthfeel," Lee writes.

Wine changes in China

Lee's upcoming third book, "The Growth and History of Fine Wine," is a business and marketing book about the fine wine industry in China, including Hong Kong, over 30 years.

Wine is becoming a new social currency, which replaces abalone and bird's nest to show respect, Lee says.

很难相信眼前这个优雅、自信又爽朗的女人已过了 50 岁。紧绷的皮肤，曼妙的身材，清澈的眼神让她看上去最多 30 多岁。看来，红酒驻颜不仅是个传说。

视频是免费的，可听她一个半小时的葡萄酒课要花差不多 2000 元人民币。即使是这样，每堂课都会被抢售一空，学生里的绝大部分是听不懂她英语的中国人。

"我曾无数次地幻想，要是我是中国人，中文足够棒，那该有多好。" Debra 说道。

上过她一次课之后，我明白，Debra 靠的不是语言。

离开课还有半小时，我早早地到了教室，里面只有 Debra 一个人。

她一边闻着课桌上每一个品酒用的酒杯，检查有没有异味，边和我打招呼。她竟然记得我的名字，而我刚和她认识不到一个小时，所谓的认识也就是一个照面。在课堂上，她能叫出每一个刚刚认识的学生的名字。

It also changes the way Chinese do business.

"It used to be about drinking baijiu (Chinese distilled spirit) and gan bei (toasting) but this has changed," Lee says. "Compared with opening a Maotai, a bottle of Lafite shows that people are more sophisticated. And the whole dining experience slows down, it's calmer due to the low alcohol content in wine."

The Chinese wine palate remains unchanged, however, and the preference is still for medium-full bodied Cabernet, she observes. One reason is that local wine producers occupy 75 percent of domestic market and they use and market Cabernet grapes. The Bordeaux region is also considered high-status. Another reason is that Chinese like strong-tasting beverages.

Q & A

Q: How do you get into wine?

A: When I studied at Oxford as an exchange student ... fine wine is always served at a formal dinner. When I touched fine wine for the first time, I was surprised wine could have so many flavors, giving the quite-plain British food flavor, just like seasoning.

Q: How do you stay objective? Do you ever award 100 points?

A: When judging a wine, it's not whether I like it or not but whether this wine possess all the characters that make a great wine. Yes (100), but rarely. It was a 1952 Chateau Lafleur, a wine that you can't describe because it's an experience, trying to explain the feeling like falling in first love.

Q: What's your wine philosophy?

A: It's just wine. Don't make such a big deal out of it. Wine can bring you joy and happiness but truly in life, there're many things more important than wine. Wine is a luxury. Luxury only comes when everything else around you, family, career, health are happy.

整堂课就像是一台由她导演的舞台剧，舞台中央放着她准备的各种各样看上去和葡萄酒无关的道具，国王的权杖，皇后的后冠，一条跳芭蕾舞时穿的蓬蓬裙。

当介绍长相思时，她又给两个学生们穿上了夏威夷草裙，用来解释这种白葡萄酒独有的青草香气。

话题转到经典的波尔多，她请了一男一女上台，一个手持权杖，一个戴上后冠：

"这位男同学就像是拉图庄，阳刚，充满力量！那位女同学就像是玛歌庄，高雅而温柔。"

当学生们向她抱怨，法国一些子产区的名字及其酒多变的风格太难记时，她说："请你们记住我家里的三只猫，其中有两只是母的，一只叫 Musigny（勃艮第东部的一个村庄，以出产酒体轻颜色浅的黑品诺而出名），另一只叫 Beaujolais（勃艮第南部产区，以出产容易入口的佳美葡萄酒而出名）。"

她可不是打比方，她真有三只领养的猫！

在男性占主导的葡萄酒世界，Debra 凭借女性的身份，意外地获得了一席之地。

"女人不太容易让人有距离感。学生们有不懂的都愿意问我，尤其是男生，爱面子的他们可不愿意在同性面前展现出他们的弱势。"Debra 说道。

她不认为自己是个葡萄酒讲师，而是个兼职做教育的葡萄酒玩家。

"葡萄酒本来就是好玩的、好喝的，干嘛把它搞得那么严肃，遥不可及！我人生最大的快乐和追求就是把这种文化去精英化。"Debra 说道。

但她考取"葡萄酒大师"这个学位，一点也不好玩。

Debra 说着一口流利的广东话，还有一点不太标准的普通话，吃着道地的中餐，视自己为中国的一部分。为了《上海葡萄酒行业指南》，她先后拜访了上海 40 家葡萄酒商店、20 多个侍酒师及他们的酒单。

从 2002 年开始，她花了整整六年考取了葡萄酒大师，通过了号称世界上最残酷的考试之一。

"终于考完了，这太痛苦了！" Debra 回忆道。

考试分为理论、品酒和论文三大部分。

理论考试，主要考核学生对于酒庄、葡萄园管理及酿酒技术的掌握。虽然 Debra 谦虚地说道，这部分能顺利通过大大出乎她的意料之外，但翻看她的履历，通过是必然。

Debra 出生于美国著名的葡萄酒产区 Sonoma，家里拥有一个小型的酒庄。长大后，她还去智利采收葡萄，去波尔多学习剪枝，去南非学习酿酒，在美国纽约附近的手指湖产区管理酒窖。

Edu-tainer: Man in tutu 'describes' Reisling

DEBRA Meiburg, the first Master of Wine (MW) in Asia, compares herself to a glass of Pinot Noir, "flirty, fruity and lively but with a solid core of serious intent."

Meiburg, an American whose family had a small hobby vineyard in Sonoma County, moved to Hong Kong 25 years ago and is now a permanent resident and noted wine educator and writer.

She says her great pleasure is educating Chinese people about wine.

"Many times I have wished I were Chinese," says Meiburg, when asked if being a Westerner makes it difficult for Chinese to relate to her message. She does

为期四天的品酒考试如地狱一般恐怖，每天 12 杯酒，四天，48 杯。每杯酒，Debra 都被要求在 10 分钟内准确地写出产地、酿酒技术、葡萄品种、陈酿时间及其市场表现。

"这意味着我只有 30 秒的时间去找寻答案，一分钟去判断，剩余的时间就是拼命地写，不然绝对来不及。我有一半靠猜，这样紧迫的品酒真不舒服。"她回忆道。

最终，她的一篇名为"中国大陆和香港葡萄酒教育市场比较分析"的论文为这六年画上了句号。之所以选择这个角度是因为 Debra 于 26 年前跟着她的老公移居并长住香港，一直活跃于两岸葡萄酒领域，对两地市场非常的熟悉。

这篇论文之后，Debra 深受启发，出版了一系列有中国视角的葡萄酒市场分析报告，包括不久前刚出版的《上海葡萄酒行业指南》。

speak Cantonese like a local, however, her Mandarin is admittedly not very good.

One of only four Masters of Wine in Asia and one of only two female MWs in Asia, she earned her degree in 2008.

Before that, she had been involved in wine industry for 15 years: She worked a harvest in Chile, pruned vines in Bordeaux, ran a grape crusher and de-stemmer in South Africa, and worked as a cellar hand in the Finger Lakes region of New York.

Today Meiburg is one of the most popular and influential wine educators in China, especially in Shanghai, where her wine-teaching video titled "Grape Moments" is aired on screens in thousands of taxis.

"I am teaching all the taxi drivers," Meiburg says with a laugh.

She also conducts wine training and appreciation courses for companies across Asia, for example, financial services companies that need to wine and dine clients.

一个老外凭什么代表中国视角？业内有很多人是不屑的。毕竟有太多来到中国的所谓国际葡萄酒大师，摆着一副高尚文化传教士的姿态。他们一方面对中国味蕾、国产酒和消费市场高谈阔论，一方面却根本不愿意也不屑于去观察和了解这方土地和人。

"上海快要追上香港了，这里的文化更包容，也更具开拓精神。"Debra 说道。

她认为，土地面积紧张是香港葡萄酒发展的一处硬伤，寸土寸金所带来的高运营成本必然导致相对保守的市场。三个月前，她在上海竟然发现有一家店专卖南非的酒，这在香港是无法想象的。

然而，无论是香港还是大陆，中餐与葡萄酒的困难融合才是阻碍葡萄酒发展的最大障碍。

"葡萄酒和美食是相互依存的，两者唯有在一起，才能迸发出火花，创造出第三维度的味觉享受。"Debra 希望能有所突破，但眼前的问题很棘手。

Her video teaching series "Meet the Winemaker," will be aired soon on youku.com.

Meiburg attributes her success to her female identity.

"The industry is traditionally dominated by men. As a female, no one is afraid of me. They don't worry about

their pride and are willing to ask me questions. Men especially are sometimes intimidated in front of other men," the wine master explains.

She likes to call herself a wine "edu-tainer."

"Wine education is entertaining. Learning should be fun," Meiburg said last month at a wine seminar in Shanghai hosted by Lucaris, an Asian crystal brand.

Her teaching style is lively and interactive, and outside of Hong Kong there's much less emphasis on language, since she's not fluent

在西餐的宴席中，海鲜因为相对清淡，基本上都搭配着白葡萄酒在上半场上场，这样才不会抢了口味较重的肉食和红酒的味道。但中餐里，海鲜，像蒸鱼、炸虾多数以热菜、大菜的姿态在后半场上场。

"你让中国人怎么习惯边吃热的鱼肉边喝冰过的白葡萄酒呢，这太奇怪了！" Debra 的一番话让很多国人感同身受。

西餐，一道菜配一杯酒。一桌中餐，单是开胃菜就可能同时有七八道在桌上，味道还各不一样。要是按西餐的逻辑，一场中式宴席最起码要 20 款酒。

Debra 的解决方案是求同存异：

"你就挑一瓶酒去配一道最爱的菜，其他的，照旧，该喝茶还是喝茶。举个例子，当鲜美的鲍鱼上桌，那代表是时候开一瓶勃艮第了。"

Debra 曾经和朋友一起做过一场勃艮第特级庄的垂直品鉴。每一瓶酒代表他们各自的出生年份，跨度从 1955 年到 1990 年。

in Mandarin. When she teaches the grape variety Riesling, a big, tall, muscular man in a ballerina's tutu steps to the platform. The reason: "Because Riesling is delicate and very beautiful but strong in the middle," Meiburg explains.

When teaching Sauvignon Blanc, she produces a person wearing a grassy hula skirt to emphasize the grassy, vegetal aroma of the wine.

When she describes Chateau Margaux, a Bordeaux wine estate, a woman in the audience dons a queen's crown and red velvet cloak, expressing the wine's femininity, elegance and status.

"This approach makes it easy for students to remember vividly," says Meiburg.

Lynne Sherriff, former chairman of the Institute of Masters of Wine, considers Meiburg's comparison of wine with people and her visual approach very useful in wine education.

"If you hear and see at the same time, that sends much stronger information to the brain," says Sheriff.

在 Debra 看来，葡萄酒创造出了一种融合历史、文化、地理和科学的美的享受。有机会的话，尝遍世界每个产区。如果觉得味道不好，等上个十年，再尝一次，或许又是新的惊艳。

When explaining wine regions, Meiburg talks about four stray cats she adopted, including one named Musigny, a commune in the Cote-d'Or department, eastern France, and another called Beaujolais, an AOC in southern Burgundy.

Earning the title Master of Wine was the most serious challenge she had faced. It's notoriously difficult.

Starting in 2002, she spent six years passing various examinations on the way to her Master of Wine degree.

Each year, only two or three people pass the international exam, which includes sections on theory and tasting as well as a dissertation.

The theory part wasn't too hard for her. It covered knowledge about owning a winery, running a vineyard and making wine.

The most difficult part was the four-day tasting. Twelve glasses of wine, red and white, are tasted each day. Candidates have 10 minutes per glass, to taste and write one and a half pages about where the wine is from, the grape variety, how it is made, aged and marketed.

"Actually, you only have 30 seconds to identify, one minute to be sure, and rest of the time to write, otherwise you cannot finish," Meiburg recalls.

Her dissertation was on wine education and training in China. Meiburg has launched a series of books and articles, mainly insider reports with in-depth analysis of the Chinese wine market.

"After becoming a Master of Wine, I am always thinking of how to make a proper business model for all the things I want to do from my heart," Meiburg says.

Her latest book, "Guide to the Shanghai Wine Trade," will be released in November. It is based on interviews with 20 sommeliers and visits to 40 wine stores.

"Come on Hong Kong, Shanghai is getting ahead of you," she says.

Early on, people in both Shanghai and Beijing didn't know about anything except Bordeaux, but times have changed. Three months ago, she found a store in Shanghai featuring exclusively South African wines; she hasn't seen such a store in Hong Kong.

Compared with Beijing, Shanghai is more experimental and open-minded, so people drink more diverse wines, she observes.

"The space in Hong Kong is also expensive, which forces its wine market to be more conservative," she adds.

The retail market in Shanghai is more robust than in Hong Kong and home consumption is much higher.

"It's probably due to different life habits. Young, wealthy Shanghai people are accustomed to dining at home, while Hong Kong people prefer to dine out," the master says.

Her observations are supported by Jerry Liao, managing sommelier at Jing'an Shangri-La, West Shanghai.

"Shanghai's wine market has been mature due to good market segmentation. Some wine traders are devoted exclusively to selling wines from a very small region," Liao says.

Wine pairing is one of the most important ways to spread wine knowledge and culture in China, Meiburg says.

"When serving food with wine, the two together create a new flavor, a third experience," she says.

But the dining habits and taste of Chinese people are totally different from those of Westerners, making wine pairing more difficult. For example, seafood is served first in the West, so that the accompanying, light, chilled white wine is served before heavier red.

However, in a typical Chinese banquet, fish is usually a hot dish served in the middle or at the end of the meal.

"It's an unfamiliar sensation for the Chinese palate to have a very cold drink with a hot, fresh fish," says Meiburg.

Furthermore, Westerners typically smell the wine, drink a bit and then have a bite of food, while Chinese usually eat first and drink wine later to wash it down, Meiburg observes. This may come from the Chinese tea-drinking tradition.

Clearly, it's impossible to transplant Western concepts in China.

One bottle on the table, one beautiful dish, one special moment - that's Meiburg's approach for Chinese dining, which she calls the relatively best solution so far.

"Pick one important dish and that's when the wine comes. The rest of the time you can drink tea, water and anything you like. For example, when the abalone arrives, you open your beautiful Burgundy," Meiburg explains.

Q & A

Q: What's your wine philosophy?

A: Wine is about history, culture, geography, science and, above all, pleasure. Try every wine region once. If it's bad, wait 10 years and try it again.

Q: How does wine touch your heart?

A: It starts in the glass. All that wonderful aroma and texture is impossible not to fall in love with, but you really fall in love when you learn all about where it came from and who the people behind it are.

Q: What's the biggest frustration in your wine life?

A: Mainly it's to do with time, especially in a new market like ours. There are so many incredible opportunities to pursue but nobody to tell you how to manage all of them.

Q: What's your impressive wine memory?

A: A wine tasting, during which well-aged Grand Cru Burgundy represents everyone's birth year, from 1955 to 1990.

231/247

"红酒客"
不差钱的
卖酒之道

红酒客董事长吴文峰刚步入 50 岁。他的一个媒体好友曾经这样评价：他是一个典型的上海商人，相对保守，也不是那么野心勃勃，但稳扎稳打，非常实惠。

这样的个性也许很难让他在挤破头的竞争环境中处于有利地位，但他恰恰因此而在这场历时数年，至今仍未结束，没有硝烟却充满腥风血雨的中国葡萄酒网络战争中得以幸免。

Wine entrepreneur unlocking market key

伟大的企业，不一定是成功的，但却有着非凡的生命力，最典型的莫过于美国电子商务公司先驱亚马逊，成立十年，仍没盈利。红酒客，中国最早致力于葡萄酒电子商务的网络平台。董事长吴文峰的梦想，就是把红酒客打造得像亚马逊一样深入人心。

在被传统销售渠道垄断的葡萄酒市场，电商的出现像是掀起了一场关于葡萄酒消费的民主革命。传统领域，无论是在葡萄酒零售店还是超级市场，卖方与买方所掌握的信息相互之间是不对等的。穿着体面的销售人员带着笑容殷勤地向顾客推荐着这瓶得过大奖，那瓶都说好喝；背后是卖方颐指气使地向消费者叫嚷着你该喝什么。但在信息爆炸的网络世界，人们可以搜索每瓶酒背后的故事及喝过的人的评价，更重要的，同时比较不同经销商的价格。

有些酒卖得贵，因为消费者要为高额的税收，一层又一层供应商的转手和卖场的入场费买单，有些酒则因为多种原因卖得很便宜。于是，消费从被动转化成主动，变成了"我想喝什么"。习近平主席的反腐决心使得葡萄酒在餐饮场所及礼品市场的销售大受打击。曾经，拉菲、拉图那些名庄酒是中国富豪的最爱。对某一人群而言，喝的早就不是酒，是面子。在中国的二三线城市，甚至出现过把一瓶瓶拉菲倒进浴缸里来炫耀财富的疯狂场面。

很长一段时间以来，红酒都是公款消费的大头，酒桌上谈生意一直是中国的传统。在那样的繁荣光景，一个葡萄酒进口商区域销售总监的年薪可以达到 300 万。虽然传统销售渠道仍然占据中国超过 85% 的市场份额，但风光不再。根据全球最权威的葡萄酒产业研究机构 Vinexpo 的统计，在连续十几年以每年25% 的比例疯狂增长后，中国的葡萄酒消费于 2013 年开始出现了下降。

"亏本卖酒在中国的电商市场太普遍了。他们赚钱靠的不是卖酒，而是忽悠风投。"吴文峰说道。

葡萄酒业内人士寄希望电商领域来拯救这个低迷的市场，因为选择电商的是看重性价比的个人消费者，是块未被填满的市场空白。一时间风起云涌，新的电商层出不穷，新老之间竞争激烈，谁都想分上一杯羹。可伴随而来的是水货泛滥，假货横行。电商之间价格战、口水仗、互相拆台，遍体鳞伤。

价格战已经到了亏本赚吆喝的地步。一瓶澳大利亚 2013 年份的黄尾袋鼠，也买酒上卖 79 元，网酒网上立刻变成了 69 元。算一笔账：通过国际权威的比价系统 wine searcher 获得这瓶酒在各个国家的售价，其中在其原产地澳大利亚销售的平均价格约为 64 元。任何一瓶酒进口到中国，都要被征收 48.2% 的关税。很明显，网酒网是亏本在卖。类似的案例不胜枚举。

CHARLES Wu, chairman and CEO of winekee.com, the first and arguably most experienced wine B2C website in China, believes the key to his survival is never positioning his company as an e-commerce provider.

The Chinese wine industry, which has relied to a large extent on government entertainment, has suffered since President Xi Jinping launched his anti-corruption policy in 2012.

After a decade of uninterrupted growth of about 25 percent annually, Chinese wine consumption paused in 2013 for the first time, dropping 2.2 percent, according to this month's report by Vinexpo Asia-Pacific, Asia's largest wine expo.

吴文峰给我描绘了一张中国特色的电商营运流程图。首先，电商把自己包装成一个差不多叫做"葡萄酒电子销售，向大众售卖优雅生活方式"的性感项目，呈现在风投面前去吸引第一轮融资。拿到这笔钱，就开始烧钱大打价格战，把价格降到市场最低，吸引消费者，抢占市场份额。接着，把市场份额数据拿到风投面前去，转而引来第二轮的风投。如果运气好，还能拿到第三轮，泡沫就这样越滚越大。这解释了在过去的几年间，涌入的风投资金如何让一家又一家葡萄酒电商成为新闻头条，不是宣称中国第一就是中国最大。可泡沫总有被戳破的那天，就像美国 2000 年互联网泡沫破裂，资金停止流动，网站接连破产，整个行业走向衰败。

"这种典型体现互联网思维的运营模式是很危险的，如果你得不到第二、第三轮风投，资金链就会断裂，你会死得很惨。"吴文峰意味深长地说。

Now industry insiders are placing their hopes on e-commerce targeting individual customers, a segment that has maintained rapid growth. With a very small base, the marketing share of e-commerce has increased continuously, ranging from 5 percent to 10 percent, according to insider reports. But there are serious problems lurking as the sites compete hard on price, the 49-year-old entrepreneur pointed out during an interview with Shanghai Daily in his Shanghai office.

A bottle of Yellow Tail 2013 Shiraz (a popular wine in Australia) sells for 69 yuan (US$11) at wangjiu.com. Wine Searcher (the world's most authoritative wine price comparing system) shows that it is sold for 64 yuan in Australia. Given that China's mainland tariff on bottled wine is 48.2 percent, wangjiu.com clearly is selling the wine at a loss.

236

"Selling wine at a loss is so popular in the Chinese e-commerce industry," Wu says. "E-commerce providers don't rely on making money from all of their wine, but market wine as a 'sexy' product to attract the first round of VC (venture capital). They use that to win the price war and contend for market share that is persuasive enough to attract the second round of VC."

The money coming from VC firms, which invest based on the potential to sell wine to China's huge consumer market, leads to e-commerce providers making headlines, boasting that they are "the biggest e-commerce wine provider in China."

"This business model is highly risky," says Wu. "If the company can't get the third round of VC, it will die."

Although Wu declines to comment on his competitors, the news of yesmywine.com, China's biggest e-commerce wine provider, suffering from a lack of venture capital is on the lips of wine professionals.

他并没有正面去评论那些竞争对手，但中国最大的红酒电商平台"也买酒"面临资金断裂的新闻不绝于耳。截至目前为止，这个泡沫仍然没有被完全戳破的迹象。这很大程度上得益于中国庞大的人口基数，12亿人口，市场太大，即使每人每年只花一百块钱买酒，那消费额也是个天文数字，把这块庞然大饼全部分光，还有待时日。

这场惨烈的战争并没有止步于电商和电商之间，电商和传统销售渠道之间，已是水火不容。进口商大骂电商扰乱市场价格秩序，认为这样的跌价根本就是要流氓。一瓶酒，在超市里可能卖三四百元左右，网上却只卖一半的价格，消费者会选贵的，除非他是傻子。和倚老卖老的传统渠道斗，年轻的电商总是吃亏的。从中国开放葡萄酒进口到现在，那么多年下来，传统线下渠道，尤其是各大进口商早就牢牢把持着主流酒的进货来源。市场份额统计也很说明问题，即使是不景气的2013、2014年，电商所占的比例仍然不到百分之十。更现实的问题是，现在多数的电商没有自己的进货渠道，而是向传统的进口商购买。若是有一天，进口商关闭了这扇门，电商很有可能会面临有市无货的窘境。

That also leads to e-commerce and the brick-and-mortar wine industry facing off. Wholesalers and retail shops accuse the online sellers of fixing the price too low and raiding the market.

Winekee.com, founded in April 2006, has never raised venture capital. It has maintained a 70 percent annual growth in turnover in the last four years.

This year, ASC, China's largest wine importer, chose winekee as one of its six authorized sellers of DBR Lafite, which owns Chateau Lafite Rothschild among other Lafite names.

The company also became the second authorized seller of Concha Y Toro (Latin America's largest wine producer) in China.

Wu attributes his success to his never positioning winekee as an e-commerce provider but instead as a wine importer and distributor.

"E-commerce for me is just a selling tool, which is more vibrant than traditional retail channels," he says.

吴文峰对此置身事外："红酒客从2006年成立至今，没有引进过风投，我们根本就没有融资压力。这只是我的 side business，一个爱好。"

他这番举重若轻倒是印证了葡萄酒电商行业里的人对红酒客的评价：这家公司很低调，成立很早，似乎从来都不缺钱。

吴文峰，不差钱。他是个出生于上海的实业家，主要涉及的领域是矿产和工程建筑，在南美有着相当大的产业，喜欢上红酒缘因当年财大硕士毕业后去加利福尼亚读MBA。

"我想，任何一个人，在加州这地方，都会自然而然地爱上葡萄酒的吧！"吴文峰说道。

他想做一些与葡萄酒相关的生意，就在那时遇上了他的好朋友 Rich Bergsund，wine.com 的 CEO。Wine.com 是一家位于旧金山的葡萄酒电商，也是全美最大的电子平台之一。吴文峰深受启发，但并没有把这套模式照搬到中国，毕竟 wine.com 借助风投烧了一亿多美金才开始盈利。

He keeps his prices low by importing wine himself, cutting out the middleman, except for a few he sources from big distributors such as ASC. The wines he directly imports contribute to 80 percent of his company's annual profit.

He has assembled a competitive management team to build relationships directly with wineries, which eases the financial strain and marketing.

The average age of his vice presidents is 30. All of them have overseas backgrounds, which helps their communication with wine producers.

"We are given long payment terms and can often invite winemakers and vintners to support our wine tasting," says the CEO.

Winekee is also the first and only B2C wine website in China with both Chinese and English versions. That helps expats, who often lack options in buying wine at reasonable prices.

"It's also part of our marketing," Wu says. "The language barrier results in many Western wineries suffering from being unable to know how their wine and brand operates in China."

电商只是个比传统门店超商更具活力的销售手段，吴文峰对自己的定位是兼具葡萄酒进口商和批发商。

过去的四年，很多国内的葡萄酒电商入不敷出地烧钱筹钱，红酒客却保持了每年70%的增长，并从前年开始盈利。吴文峰把成功归因于从来没有把自己定位成电商。

一直以来，吴文峰都在用经营实业的思维方式经营着红酒客。价格的劣势，吴文峰试图从根本上去解决。虽然他也从进口商那里买酒，是国内最大进口商ASC的大客户，但他逐渐把这块比重降低，如今他自己进口的酒占网站销售量的百分之八十。

做进口商并不是件容易的事情，需要获得欧美葡萄酒生产商的信任，语言及思想上的无障碍沟通显得尤为重要。这从某种程度上也解释了ASC，一个美国人创立的公司在中国的成功。吴文峰组建了一支年轻的管理团队，副总裁的平均年龄才30左右，但都有留学海外的背景，有在法国波尔多读葡萄酒的，也有在美国读商的。这样的团队结构，除了获得越来越多的代理权，像是拉菲酒庄的母公司DBR，拉丁美洲最大的葡萄酒产商Concha Y Toro，还让红酒客获得了比其他公司更长的付款期，缓解了资金周转的压力。

Spot the trend

The Shanghai-born entrepreneur showed what may have been a shrewd business sense in the last several years. Many wine companies were blindly pursuing Bordeaux first growths (the highly expensive cream of the crop of Bordeaux wines), especially Chateau Lafite and Chateau Latour, which are popular among government officials. But Wu targets middle and low-end wines to attract private wine lovers.

"I didn't think that kind of distorted wine consumption would last for a long time. How can you imagine the wife of a police inspector in a small Chinese town, also the owner of a restaurant selling wine, undertakes the government entertainment of the whole town!" says the businessman.

He says that the wine-consuming power in China is moving to the increasingly large middle class — people who are well-educated and pursuing quality of life.

但即使如此，降低成本还是比不上竞争对手的亏本卖。吴文峰的思路是，若价格不够给力，服务来补齐，从单纯意义上的卖酒，演变成卖一种葡萄酒的体验。他和携程合作推出了酒庄之旅。客人可以享有特权去参观不对外开放的酒庄，看他们的葡萄园，甚至喝到些不公开发售的神秘之酒。

"以我的经验，如果一个客人去过这个酒庄，他／她对这个酒庄的忠诚度是一辈子的，虽然这样的效果不是立竿见影，但后劲可观。"吴文峰认为。

他还把网站做成了中英文两个版本。表面上看，是为了满足在上海生活工作的老外对葡萄酒的需求，这块市场购买力虽强，但基数有限，其实他还有一层考虑，完善其对上层供应商的服务，让他们心里舒服。吴文峰的这个做法，算得上是电商领域的超前一步。

"Their (middle class) consumption concept is now at a turning point, from drinking wine to enjoying good wine. They expect to know more about the wine, including the vineyard and winemaker behind the bottle. It's a natural change after three to five years' drinking experience," he says.

Under that new situation, Chinese are beginning to select their wines based more on palate than label. Wu anticipates that Chilean wine, known for its smooth character and reasonable price, may be as popular as French wine in the near future.

"We (Chinese) deeply appreciate smoothness and directness, which can be proved by our loving baijiu (distilled spirit made from sorghum)," says Wu.

According to the Shanghai Customs, France occupies 45.4 percent of China's imported wine by volume, with Chile in a distant second place with 11.9 percent in the first quarter of this year.

Wu is now working with ctrip.com, one of the nation's biggest travel agencies, to launch a Chilean wine tour.

我在国外参观酒庄的时候，庄主们无不表达了一种顾虑：在他们把酒卖给中国的进口商之后，就像是石沉大海，或是说两眼一抹黑。天知道他们到底以什么价格在中国市场上卖，又是以怎样的方式向中国消费者宣传他们的酒庄。是暴发户的首选呢还是优雅的代名词呢？是强调他们的风土还是酿造？这些都不得而知。英文网站的建立让一切都变得更为透明，很大程度上克服了这些酒庄对于未知的恐惧。

"If customers have been to the winery, meeting the vintner and strolling along the vineyards, they usually have a lifelong loyalty to that wine," Wu says.

One of Wu's friends calls him "a textbook Shanghainese businessman, comparatively conservative, not too aggressive, steady and pragmatic."

Most local wine professionals barely know of winekee. Their general impression is that it's low-profile, rarely making headlines.

"It's a company having survived in the wine industry for a long time. Strangely, it seems to be never pressed for money," says Roger Hou, co-founder of wineyun.com, an e-commerce provider based in Shanghai.

Wu's personal background may be the cause of the confusion.

"It is inherently my side business, my hobby," he says.

吴文峰早早地认识到，主导中国市场的消费力量，势必或是已经转向了日益强大的中产阶级，这批人有着良好的教育背景，追求生活品质。相比酒标上的名字，他们更看重酒瓶里的味道值不值这价钱。

上海有句俚语：要懂得看山水。意思是说，要对周遭的人和环境保持一份敏锐，并作出快速的反应。看得懂山水，见风使舵，那就掌握了主动，成为赢家。

上海商人吴文峰深谙此道，因而他的葡萄酒事业没有怎么受到反腐大潮的冲击。在 2009 到 2012 年期间，众多酒商，无论线上线下，一窝蜂地狂热追捧公务宴请最爱的波尔多名庄，无论多高的价格都拼命囤货，指望着 2000 块的酒一转手就能变成 10000 块，就因为那些贪官用国家的钱一点也不手软。他却把目光转向了些旧世界中低端的和新世界出产的那些性价比高的酒，比如智利。

"你能想象吗？那时一个县城的公安局局长老婆会专门开个餐厅去卖酒，承包了这个县所有的公务消费。我不认为这种畸形的腐败会继续下去，更民主更廉洁的政党是这个时代的主流和必然趋势。"吴文峰说道。

Wu is mainly involved in construction and mining equipment. His passion for wine started in 1990, when he graduated from Shanghai University of Finance and Economics with a master's degree in economics and flew to the US, studying for his MBA in international finance at California State University, Fullerton.

"People, including me, fall in love with wine in California naturally," he says.

Together with his partners, who are all local media people, Wu established winekee.com eight years ago. It was originally a simple website for people to share their wine experiences. Starting in 2009, the company transformed itself into a wine e-seller. The inspiration came from Wu's friend, Rich Bergsund, CEO at wine.com, a San Francisco-based e-commerce wine provider that sources wine from importers and has a just-in-time inventory system.

从 2013 年开始，中国葡萄酒行业的日子就没那么好过了，关掉的电商，破产的进口商，离职的侍酒师，前景似乎一片黯淡。但吴文峰看到的"山水"却不是这样，觉得这个行业在国内的发展才刚刚开始。他有一个颇为大胆的预测：中国总有一天会超越美国成为全球最大的葡萄酒市场。

"只不过，"他停留了片刻，"中国人对于'明天'有太多的期待，总想着能在一夜之间改变一切。可是，什么事情都得一步步来，这个世界原本如此。"

吴文峰也不见得就是这个时代的葡萄酒赢家，当泡沫戳破，博弈才刚刚开始。

Wu didn't simply copy that model, but adapted it, particularly drawn to the idea of importing himself and limiting the scale. He says that wine.com "burned more than 1 billion dollars" before it started making a profit.

He's optimistic of his side business and thinks China will surpass America to be the biggest wine market in the world. The war for wine business is just beginning.

Wu's favorite wine is Chateau Monbousquet, a Saint-Emilion grand cru classe Bordeaux, that is thick, complex and balanced.

Merits to both business models

The dispute between traditional wine retailers and e-commerce never stops. Stephen Li, China's leading wine educator and a Master of Wine candidate, analyzes their advantages and disadvantages.

Price and convenience make e-commerce competitive. Without the slotting allowance and rental fee, wine sold on a website can be much cheaper. E-commerce's home delivery service saves customers time and labor.

However, the logistics can be a big problem. Some e-commerce companies have destroyed wine by shipping bottles across the country with huge temperature differences between areas. Bottles exploding at freezing temperatures and wine deteriorating in hot areas are common.

Traditional retail, represented by supermarkets and wine shops, has its advantages. Customers can sometimes taste wine before buying it, and corked wine can easily be exchanged or returned.

1. 也买酒 www.yesmywine.com

也买酒成立于 2008 年 6 月，目前为中国规模最大的葡萄酒电商，总部位于上海。目前网站也拥有 700 多万会员，售卖 8000 多款产品，平均每天售出 23 万瓶酒。除了卖酒，也买酒也从事葡萄酒教育，现为 WSET 授权培训机构。

2. 酒云网 www.wineyun.com

网站成立于 2014 年，总部位于上海，前身为酒射闪购，在专业葡萄酒爱好者中颇受欢迎。营业规模不大，以小众精品酒为主。与别家葡萄酒电商最大的不同是其只提供闪购模式从而维持价格优势，即限时限量特卖。

3. 网酒网 www.wangjiu.com

网站成立于 2011 年 10 月，总部位于北京。

4. 酒仙网 www.jiuxian.com

网站成立于 2013 年 9 月，总部位于北京，除葡萄酒外也经营白酒、洋酒、啤酒等等。

中国最具影响力葡萄酒电商

251
267

侍酒师
为何
开精品酒店

他是全世界最有声望的侍酒师。位于英国南部 Hotel TerraVina 是 Gerard 开的以葡萄酒为主题的精品酒店。慕名而来的人们对 Gerard，这个全世界唯一同时拿到葡萄酒大师、侍酒师大师、葡萄酒 MBA 三个头衔的传奇人物充满期待。

Breaking
the stereotype of
'haughty' wine
steward

相传在中国安徽境内云雾缭绕的黄山生活着一只小蜘蛛。它每天几乎只做一件事情，吐丝织网。好不容易织好，可山里湿气重，一滴露水把网戳破。它只能重新再织一张。偏偏那天刮了大风，网又破了，小蜘蛛没有放弃，再织一张。隔天，山里又下了场雨，网又破了，就这样破了又织，织了又破，循环往复。

那只小蜘蛛，活脱脱就是今年 57 岁 Gerard Basset 的人生缩影。Hotel TerraVina 是一栋漂亮的红砖小楼，带有经典欧洲 18 世纪的建筑风格。内部的装饰，从墙面到地板几乎都选用了原木，不仅让人倍感温馨，也很好地映衬了酒店所在位置。那片区域叫 New Forest，被当地华裔翻译为新森林。早在一千年前，这地方就很漂亮，到处都是参天大树，灌木丛中点缀着野花，生活着各种野生动物，被当时的英国国王威廉一世一眼相中，成为了他的狩猎场。如今，这里已成为英国的国家公园，到处可见人们悠闲地散步、骑车，是户外运动胜地。

酒店不大，因而总是熙熙攘攘的，人们多是慕名而来，希望能尝到最好喝的葡萄酒，吃到最天然有机的食物。也有些回头客并不知道 Gerard 是谁，只是觉得这个带有明显高卢人长相，说着带有法国口音英语的老板很特别。他侍酒的时候，散发出一种让人觉得舒服、亲近、安全的气场。客人即使对葡萄酒的文化浑然不知，甚至连酒杯都不会拿，也没有丝毫被怠慢的感觉。相反地，你越是不懂酒，他越是在乎你。

这恰恰是他刚刚获得 Decanter 杂志年度人物的原因。这个奖项，一年一次，面向全世界，只授予对全球葡萄酒行业产生决定性变革和深远影响的人物。

"他 (Gerard) 彻底改变了人们对侍酒师这个角色的定义和偏见。曾几何时,这份职业等同于傲慢,高高在上,势利眼的法国人。自他出现,侍酒师成为守候在餐桌旁努力传递快乐和幸福的使者。"Decanter 出版总监 Sarah Kemp 说起授予他奖项的原因。

"在我眼里,每一个客人都是独一无二的。作为侍酒师,你一定要设身处地多为他们想想。尤其是那些向往葡萄酒却因为自己不懂酒而战战兢兢的客人,你在他们面前大说一通让他们听得云里雾里的产区、酒庄、葡萄酿造,你有考虑过他们的感受吗?"Gerard 说道。

尊重,是他侍酒的第一原则。这可不是出于礼貌挂上职业性的微笑,或是公式化殷勤地拉个椅子,倒个酒,而是发自内心。

French sommelier Gerard Basset, arguably the world's top wine steward, is determined to change perceptions of the disdainful Frenchman. Ruby Gao explains.

Sommelier Gerard Basset compares himself to a glass of Napa Valley Cabernet Sauvignon — persistent, tannic and yet with soft in character.

In fact, his life is an example of persistence in achieving his wine goals.

"To be a great sommelier, persistent commitment speaks louder than talent," Basset says.

Basset is arguably the world's top sommelier and he has played a leading role in changing the definition of wine service and altering the stereotype of the haughty, condescending Frenchman. His aim is to put customers at ease.

"我向来都给客人最少两种选择，若是直接告诉他们你应该喝哪一种，不就是盛气凌人地把人家逼到墙角嘛。酒单的设计也是一个道理，你若是放了百分之九十的贵酒，只剩下百分之十的便宜酒，这等于变相和那些口袋不那么富裕的客人说，这不是你该来的地方。"他进一步解释道。

经营自己的酒店终究是辛苦的，从客房、餐厅到酒窖的管理，都要亲力亲为。Gerard 倒是擅长苦中作乐。他曾经最爱做的事情就是和合伙人坐在餐厅的一角，上上下下打量来往的女客人，用各种葡萄酒对她们进行个总结。典型的法国人作风!

"现在想想有点傻哦! 我们时常会说，看，这女人多精致，像一款漂亮的雷司令，那个女人性感，如同一杯迷人的霞多丽。"他回忆道。

Gerard 的幽默感和他充满坎坷的人生形成鲜明的反差。或许这是上天对他的补偿。

The 56-year-old French wine steward achieved his wine dream in England. He is the only person to hold all three degrees — Master Sommelier (MS), Master of Wine (MW) and Wine MBA.

He was the World Champion Sommelier in 2010.

In May this year he was honored "Decanter Man of the Year," a title "given only to individuals who made a difference in the world of wine and whose influence will live on," says Sarah Kemp, publishing director of Decanter.

"我常会从台上那些落寞的面孔中去挖掘潜在的苗子。在比赛中，赢家展现的往往是天赋和才华，失败者释放出更多坚持不懈的态度。"曾经屡败屡战的 Gerard 对人才有着自己的定义。

他第一次为世人所熟知是赢得了 2010 年度世界侍酒师大赛冠军。获奖的那一刻，台下闪光灯咔嚓咔嚓此起彼伏，Gerard 被记者们拿着话筒团团围住，生怕错过他的一句感言。这是他再熟悉不过的场面。这项比赛他已参加了六次，更惨的是其中三次都是亚军，差冠军一步之遥。做千年老二的感觉远比没有入围决赛更痛苦，这其中交杂着不甘、挫败、遗憾、嫉妒、落寞等种种复杂情绪。

在屡败屡战的过程中，Gerard 曾经痛苦地徘徊于放弃和坚持之间。为筹备比赛，每天都需要全力以赴地进行高强度盲品练习，付出的时间和金钱成本太高。但若是已爬到了半山腰，几乎都能想象出山顶风景的高远和壮丽，再下山，又似乎不太甘心。

He has changed the perception of a sommelier, from the stereotypical "haughty Frenchman with his nose in the air who condescends to his customers" to being a helpful steward "at the forefront of guiding consumers to the diversity of wine, and joyfully so," Kemp explains.

"Every customer is different. It's important for a sommelier to stand in the customer's shoes, understanding them, caring about them, making them feel comfortable, especially when serving those who feel scared about wine," says Basset, who spoke to Shanghai Daily at the Jing An Shangri-La last Friday after a sommelier competition.

He sums up his wine-serving philosophy: "I always give customers more than one suggestion or they will feel backed into a corner. The wine list also shows how much you respect your customers. For example, if a list has 90 percent expensive wines and 10

"这个世界就是这么现实。当我以第二名的身份站在台上的时候，摄影记者嫌我碍眼，挡到了第一名的镜头，挥手叫我让开。得冠军的时候，我在台上整整待了一个小时。这一次，终于达成梦想。现在想想这时间点也不赖，那一年我儿子Romane11岁，到了和我分享荣耀，为他老爸骄傲的岁数。"Gerard 回忆道。

这个冠军，他做得比别人辛苦且漫长。也正因为如此，他在培养和挖掘新人时的思路与常人不同。

或许，Gerard 从失败者身上找到一种相依相惜的感觉。做他的学生无疑是幸福的。他既不会成天摆谱耍大牌，让学生找不到人，重复着那种虚伪的"加油，你一定可以"的空话，也不会如真人秀节目《地狱厨房》的 Gordon Ramsay 那样砸盘子掀桌子，一副恨铁不成钢的样子。

"我的教育方法是陪伴，和他们一起工作，一起盲品，让他们知道我不是神，不是什么一蹴而就的奇迹。盲品中，我也会错。如果像我这样平凡的人也能做到，为什么你不行呢？"Gerard 反问道。

percent affordable wines, some customers will feel embarrassed because they are forced to choose from that negligible 10 percent. It's just like telling them 'you are not part of the club'."

Many young sommeliers look up to him because of both his achievements and his modesty and approachable character.

"What I love about Gerard is that he demonstrates the same humility and curiosity today as he did when I first met him when he was a junior wine waiter at Chewton Glen in the early 1980s," says Jancis Robinson, a world-leading wine critic and a MW.

Basset has also discovered and mentored a generation of the world's leading sommeliers.

"My way of inspiring the young generation is working with them, exercising blind tasting together with them, showing them I am not magic and make mistakes as well. If I can, you can!" says the wine master.

He was in Shanghai to judge Shangri-La's first Best Sommelier Competition and to hold a one-day master class for all the Shangri-La's sommeliers.

如今的他是空中飞人，到世界各地担任侍酒师大赛的评委。只有候机的时候，才有空去查收几乎每天都被各种拜师请求挤爆的邮箱。我和他的访谈也是得益于他受香格里拉集团之邀，来上海担任侍酒师比赛的评委和技术指导。

"我不是说天赋不重要，但在葡萄酒的世界里，态度的确可以弥补先天的缺陷。这次来中国，我发现这里很多侍酒师老在嘴上空谈热情，没有实际的努力和行动，这根本就是在浪费时间。"他说道。

世界最具影响力的酒评家 Jancis Robinson 看来是真正了解 Gerard 的知己。她曾在一个公开场合说道："我之所以爱 Gerard 是因为时至今日的他仍然保持着 1980 年代初期，我第一次在 Chewton Glen（英格兰南部一家极奢华的五星级酒店）见到他时的初心。他的谦卑、幽默、亲和，还有那份对世间种种充满好奇的心态，从来没有变过。"

"你知道上海哪里有好吃的餐厅吗？"Gerard 在采访中岔开了话题。

"我知道一家在进贤路上，绝对地道，不过环境一般般。"我答道。

"下次我再来上海，能带我去吗？"他问道。

他说话的时候，眼睛直视着对方，眼神里透着笑意，语气温柔，浑身释放出令人温暖的感觉。很难想象，这样一个人的童年却是冰冷的，冷到刺骨，倍感酸楚。人们常说，我们在人前刻意展现的，往往是内心最缺乏的东西。

"We invited him not only because of his humble character and strong eagerness to learn, but also because he understands the importance of salesmanship as a sommelier. We do not see all these qualities in most Chinese sommeliers," says Lu Yang, wine director at Shangri-La Group.

As a Hong Kong-based hotel group with half of its hotels in China, Shangri-La's most sommeliers are Chinese. Basset cites Jerry Liao, who took third place, as an impressive example of the best of the young generation.

"我希望自己带给别人的是快乐，因而在学校里，时常扮演成小丑逗别人发笑。" Gerard 回忆自己的童年。

人生的天平就是那么奇妙而精准。如果 Gerard 不是出身这样一个家庭，他就不会有那一次的离家出走，紧跟着是那场改变他人生的球赛，和他踏进餐厅的第一步。

他出生于法国，自记事起每天都要看一场父母上演的互相争吵甚至动手的大戏。幼小的他因此变得脆弱、敏感、无助，甚至把父母的不和归结于自己身上。他不愿意回家，更喜欢待在学校里。

他曾经是班上成绩最优秀的孩子，尤其是数学，老拿第一。他也热衷运动，尤其是骑自行车。那时他最大的梦想就是长大了成为专业车手参加环法自行车赛。可无论在学校里他多么风光，下课后还是要回那个家，那个吵到他根本无法专心写作业的家。成绩因此一落千丈，父母也对他不闻不问。绝望中，他于16岁选择了退学，离家出走。若是无法和命运对抗，人们能做的，要么放弃初心消极服从，要么逃离原有的环境去积极寻求改变。

Liao is managing sommelier at the Jing An Shangri-La.

"He's very talented and knowledgeable in the theoretical part and he could go far. Very soon Chinese sommeliers like him will be considered qualified to compete on the world stage," Basset says.

Sommelier is still a new profession in China, he observes. "Many are enthusiastic, repeatedly talking about their 'passion,' (but) I think the word is overused. Without action and persistent commitment, it means nothing."

Right attitude

He often discovers talent in competitions and also sees promise in some people who don't take the awards. Winners show talent but some who don't win show the right attitude and ask them what mistakes they made.

那一年，稚嫩的他根本不知道自己能干些什么，就这样在法国打着零工到处漂泊。有一天，他赚了点钱，心血来潮想去英国看一场他最爱的英超联赛，支持下他喜欢的利物浦队。在踏上那片寒冷多雨的岛国的刹那，Gerard 爱上了那里。对于一个既没有学历又不会英文的法国人来说，在英国生存异常艰难。他在一家餐厅的后厨找到了份杂物工的差事。过了没多久，他的英文流利了些，餐厅升他做了服务生。老板固执地认定一个法国人比英国人更懂得美食和美酒。

"那真的是异想天开，事实上我什么也不懂。"Gerard 回忆道。

自打做服务生的第一天开始，他倒是真心喜欢上了餐饮行业。这份工作让人有成就感，只要做得好，就能带给别人饱足和快乐，这些都会迅速而直白地写在客人的脸上。雄心壮志被点燃，他去法国修读了两年厨师课程后再次回到英国，正式开启了他美食美酒的征程。他加入了 Chewton Glen，成为那里的首席侍酒师。

Basset competed for World's Best Sommelier six times until he won the first prize. In 1992, 2004 and 2007 he took second place.

"If you finish second three times, it's very frustrating not to win. It's just one step away from the first, and second means nothing," he observes.

The first time he won second place, he felt fantastic, but the second and third times, photographers wanted only the champion and asked him to get out of the shot.

When he finally won first place in 2010, he stayed for an hour on stage and his 11-year-old son Romane was old enough to share his glory.

Basset once considered giving up during those attempts, asking himself whether it was worth all the energy, time and money, however, he persevered.

Among his numerous titles, including an OBE for contributions to the hospitality industry, Basset considers the MW to be the most challenging. He attained it in 1998, nine years after he was accredited MS.

"这两年于我来说影响深远。因为有厨师的背景，我比其他侍酒师更懂得去挖掘餐酒搭配背后的种种微妙和惊喜。"他说道。

相较于侍酒师，厨师对于食物的味道、色彩、口感、香气拿捏得更为细腻、准确。这些元素和葡萄酒在口腔中融合后，每一秒都会产生细微变化或是激情碰撞。Gerard 擅长的就是捕捉并运用这种融合。

从厨房打杂开始一路走来，他清楚餐厅底层员工每天承受的辛苦和委屈，因而格外捍卫他们的利益。曾经不止一次，为不让员工受到无理刁难，他把盛气凌人的客人赶出了酒店。

The academic exams and essays were difficult because they had to be written in English, and he left school at the age of 16.

"I even cannot write an essay well in French," the master says. "That's completely alien to me."

Compared with other MW students focusing on blind tasting and improving their wine knowledge, Basset had to make special efforts to express himself in written English.

He regularly read The Economist, which is known for its well-organized, essay-like articles.

"I learned writing through analyzing the structure of each paragraph," he says. He worked out how to make his introduction and conclusion fit.

A sour beginning

Basset left school early because he was discontented and wanted a change. His parents fought every day and didn't support his aspiration to be a cyclist and win the Tour de France. He was good in math and for a time he was at the top of his class in math, but he stopped studying because he couldn't concentrate at home.

"I always acted like a clown at school to make people laugh," he says of his way of getting attention.

In 1979, he went to Liverpool for a football match, fell in love with England and moved there. As a Frenchman without skills and unable to speak English, he didn't have many choices. He became a kitchen porter.

When his English improved, he was promoted to waiter since it was assumed French people know about food and wine.

"But they're wrong. Actually I knew little," he recalls.

"我就像是一杯产自 Napa Valley（纳帕谷）的赤霞珠，丹宁强劲，生命力顽强，但仍然保持了柔软的个性。" Gerard 用一款酒总结了自己的过去。

这之后很长一段时间，Gerard 算是顺风顺水，曾经所受的教育上的断层和缺失似乎也被很好地掩盖了。直到有一天，他想考 Master of Wine（葡萄酒大师）。

这场考试和他很早就顺利通过的侍酒师大师不同。后者重视的是实践操作，前者强调理论研究，等待他的是用英文写一篇又一篇论文。

"我 16 岁就辍学，用自己的母语法文写论文都不会，更别说用英文了。"他感叹道。

但他相信精诚所至金石为开。相较于同期考试的同学，他付出额外的努力从零开始学写论文，按部就班地学习引言、主文、结论综述。

"我当时就去读 Economist（经济学人杂志）。这里面的每一篇文章几乎都是结构严谨的论文，我努力地去琢磨他们是怎么写每一个段落，怎么论述自己的观点，看一遍不行就两遍、三遍。"他回忆道。

He returned to France for a two-year chef's course and then returned to England to begin his food and wine journey.

"My chef's background was a great advantage as I began to serve wine," he says. "Since I knew how to make the food, I could explain the connection and interaction between food and wine."

In 1988 he joined Chewton Glen, a luxury hotel in Hampshire, rising to head sommelier. Then he started his marathon for various qualifications and competitions.

In 1994 Basset started his life as hotelier, cofounding Hotel du Vin in Winchester and selling it 10 years later. In 2007, he and his wife Nina opened TerraVina, a boutique hotel, in Hampshire.

从那时起，他养成了坚持阅读的习惯，直到现在。Gerard 最爱那些励志题材，总能从中获得正能量，帮助他挺过最艰难的时光。

2008 年开始，全球陷入次贷危机所引发的经济大萧条，他的酒店损失惨重，生意最冷清的时候，一天只有四个客人来用餐，一个房间也没卖出去。但是，那么多坎坷都熬过去了，这又算得上什么？

瞬间想起全球餐饮业巨子 Michael Chow 曾说过的一句话：一个厉害的人懂得回避自己的缺点，但真正的大师懂得运用自己的缺陷。

Gerard 用自己的努力实践着这个真谛。

"When establishing a hotel, many hoteliers look at the number of rooms and location, while I focus on the cellar," says Basset.

At Hotel du Vin, Basset used to sit on one side with his partner, describing attractive women as types of wine, a beautiful Riesling or a lovely Chardonnay.

He always supported his staff when they were bullied by rude customers and once banned an ill-mannered patron from his hotel.

Times have been hard since the global financial crisis hit in 2008, followed by the great recession in the euro zone.

At times there are only four customers/guests a day and no room bookings. "Probably that's because making money is not the goal my wife and I originally set."

As in his wine career, he believes persistence will pay off. "In the future I will focus more on pursuing a business success," says Basset.

269
/285

意大利酒王的
破旧立新之路

在世界酿酒史上，有一瓶酒显得尤为特别，它叫 Darmagi，意大利语，意思是太可惜。

"丢人现眼！罪大恶极！"这瓶酒被意大利人骂得体无完肤，却让全世界重新审视皮尔蒙特这块古老而又神秘的土地。这酒背后的人呼之欲出，只有王者才有这样自嘲的勇气。

意大利只有一个酒王 Angelo Gaja。

Wine with
a bold name:
'What a Shame!'

1978 年，Angelo Gaja 破天荒地在意大利种下外来葡萄品种赤霞珠。一石激起千层浪，在意大利这个传统而古老的国度，这是对本土酿酒文化的背叛和亵渎。

"当年，我的父亲看着这瓶酒摇摇头说'太可惜，糟蹋了这片美好的土地。'于是，我就想到用太可惜来命名，算是以一种幽默来向父亲致敬吧！"Angelo 回忆道。

当时酒王坐在我对面，散发着一种独特的兼具霸气和浪漫的气场。体型结实，皮肤紧实，反应之快，应对之自如，让人很难相信他已是 72 岁高龄。有意思的是，采访中，他一开始说着英文，语气平缓而温雅，情绪一上来，就自动切换到意大利语，越讲越快，音调如意大利歌剧般华丽高调。

到底是什么铸就了酒王的离经叛道？又是什么赋予了其在保守的土地上进行革新的勇气？

Angelo 出生于阿尔巴。那是位于意大利西北部的一座古老的小城，乍看上去太普通了，既没有弗洛伦萨壮美的文艺复兴建筑，也没有西西里岛那被阳光洒满的海岸线，唯一有点名气的就是当地盛产全世界最贵的食材——白松露。就是这样的一个地方，却被誉为意大利在历经二战重创之后经济发展的奇迹，短短数年，就业率飞涨，诞生了全球第四大甜品制造商费力罗。这里的空气，散发着有别于其他地方的包容和开放。

1960 年，Angelo 从阿尔巴的葡萄酒学校毕业。选择读葡萄酒，很大程度上是因为他背负着家族的使命。Gaja 酒庄于 1859 年创立，到他爸爸这里已是第三代，但却没有陷入欧洲富不过三代的宿命。相反，Angelo 的父亲瞄准了二战后一片萧条却又蓄势待发的时间点，收购了大量优质的葡萄园。摆在 Angelo 面前的已是块品质上乘的面料，就看他会把它做成高街还是高级定制了。

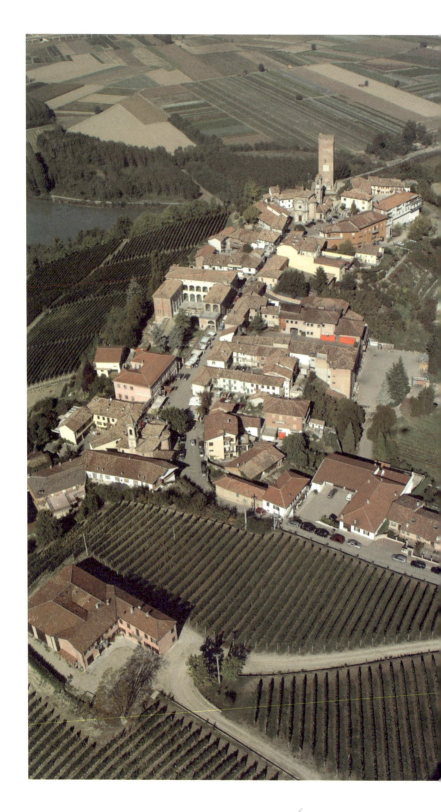

Angelo 曾经在媒体面前公开说道，和 Mondavi 的合作就如同是蚊子和大象之间的做爱，非常危险，也不舒服。

年轻的 Angelo 没有明确的想法，只能选择旅行来排空纷扰，倾听内心的声音。

他来到了伦敦，在一家速食店里打工筹措旅费。手法娴熟的 Angelo 总能将鱼块和薯条炸得金黄、均匀，油锅里发出高低起伏的滋滋声，好听极了。赚来的钱，他几乎都用在了那一家家高档餐厅里，可那里的酒单让他失望不已。厚厚的一叠，被波尔多霸占，好不容易有几款意大利酒，也是廉价的代名词，不是 Soave 就是 Chianti。

"到了国外，我才知道原来意大利根本没有存在感。" Angelo 说道。

如果说伦敦点燃了他内心谋求改变的火焰，那么在加州他找到了改变的勇气和方向。第一次去加州，他 34 岁，惊讶地发现在地球的另一端存在着与欧洲截然不同的葡萄酒理想。

Not many winemakers give their wines an unflattering names, such as "Darmagi," which means "What a Shame" in the Piedmont dialect.

Angelo Gaja, a fourth-generation vintner and innovator, is one of them, however, conferring in jest the label of Darmagi upon an Italian Cabernet Sauvignon.

That name refers to the vintner's father Giovanni Gaja, who was displeased with his son's unprecedented planting in 1978 of Cabernet Sauvignon, a non-native variety in Italy. For most local wine producers, growing a non-native grape meant betraying Italian tradition.

"'Darmagi! Planting Cabernet is such a waste of our good land,' my father said. It is my way, in a humorous tone, to commemorate my father," says the son.

他在那里遇上了老乡Robert Mondavi，一见如故。这两人有着相似的价值观。Mondavi，这个美国的第二代意大利移民，被誉为加州葡萄酒产业最重要的革新者。他冒天下之大不韪，率先把所用葡萄品种印在了酒标上。这瞬间剥去了过去千百年来葡萄酒的那层神秘的外衣，这份神秘一直成就着那些庄主、酿酒师、侍酒师们高高在上的骄傲，连带着那副让很多人望而生畏或是讨厌的"我懂，你们不懂"的姿态。

一直有传言说，Gaja和Mondavi会联手铸造新的葡萄酒奇迹。但两人之间的关系随后却发生了微妙的变化。但那已是后话了，当时的Angelo在加州被注入了一支强心剂："那里的人做葡萄酒是因为爱，而非继承。所以，他们更舍得花钱，也更勇于试验和革新去挖掘更大的可能。这地方赋予了我勇气，去追随我的初心。"Angelo回忆道。

一个身处老世界的庄主对于新世界真诚地赞美着，Angelo的心是有多大。

Gaja, owner of Gaja Winery, is probably best known as the "king of Barbaresco," who elevated a cheap, rough and undistinguished wine into the ranks of world-class wine. He is also a pioneer who dragged Piedmont winemaking into the modern world.

Gaja was recently in Shanghai to sign the Chinese translation of his book, "The Vines of San Lorenzo," the story of how he transformed obscure Barbaresco into a coveted wine for connoisseurs. The book was written by a wine lover.

"I swear I never paid for it and that's why I like it, it's not commercial, just like my fine wine," says Gaja.

The Gaja Winery in Italy's northwest Piedmont region was founded in 1858 by Giovanni Gaja, the vintner's great-grandfather. It is known for its Barbaresco and Barolo wines, both using the native varietal Nebbiolo. In 1997, Wine Spectator called Barbaresco "the finest Italian wine ever made."

Gaja is credited with developing techniques that have revolutionized winemaking in Italy. Born in Alba, he studied viticulture in both Italy and France, and became the first one in Italy to experiment with single vineyard production. He was also the first in Italy to use new French oak, instead of old oak, to age wine.

"我宁愿称自己为这片土地忠诚的守护者。所谓的改变都是为了更好地守护，去挖掘它的潜能，传承它的美好。直到现在，我仍不忘初心。"

一回到意大利，Angelo 不仅破天荒地种下了赤霞珠，还实行了许多在他父亲和当地酒农看来疯狂到像是吃错药一般的举措，比如大幅度减产。到了夏天，葡萄园里历年那茂盛的枝叶变得稀疏，和比邻的葡萄园相比，显得尤为萧条。隔壁家的农民都在偷笑，有收成却不要，和傻子没什么不同。

Angelo 至今还记得父亲一脸苦恼的表情，担忧地说："再这样减产下去，我们就要破产，付不起工人薪水了。"

与其他农作物相比，葡萄树非常不同，甚至可以说，最具人性。它有着无比旺盛的生命力，只要任其发展，葡萄藤就如同一匹脱缰的野马，枝繁叶茂，果实累累，但每棵葡萄树所享有的阳光和养分是有限的，于是，这些能量只能被稀释，来供养所有的果实。Angelo 减产的目的正是为了提高葡萄品质。

Angelo 的每一个动作对于保守的意大利来说，都是陌生而创新的。虽然农民们不待见他，但意大利媒体兴奋地追捧他为"冒险家"、"变革家"。

He is widely described as an adventurer and innovator.

"I would rather say that I am a vintner devoted to my land (Piedmont), trying to fully tap its potential and present its diverse beauty," says Gaja.

More importantly, the 73-year-old vintner has made his Barbaresco globally influential, selling it at French grand cru prices. Before that, much Italian wine was generally low cost and considered rough. That perception persists today in China.

Noted critic Julian Street (1879-1947) wrote in his book "Wines" that Italians generally dislike the important details of winemaking, considering them insignificant and trivial. They emphasize quantity rather than quality, he says.

"My efforts in making my wine merit the price," Gaja says.

"我一点也不喜欢那些称号。"
Angelo 无奈地摇摇头。

Angelo 口中的这片土地就是那神秘而古老的 Barbaresco。这是意大利最美丽的村庄之一，平缓略带陡峭的山坡上种满了一排排的葡萄，每到初夏，满眼的绿色一眼望不到边际。如果站在山坡的高处，可以看到远处连绵起伏的阿尔卑斯山。Angelo 的葡萄园就在其中的一片向阳的高坡上。在意大利当地有句俗语：最好的葡萄园永远在山上最先化雪的地方。

在世界的葡萄酒版图上，这片葡萄园的与众不同之处就是拥有当地古老而神秘的葡萄品种 Nebbiolo。

"The Chinese generalization of Italian wine as cheap is likely to last for some time. They would rather spend money on Bordeaux grand cru," he adds.

Gaja suggests that China increase its quality wine production through building its own regulated appellation system.

"Europe originated system based on a thousand years' agricultural experience clarifies gray areas of winemaking, offering a good reference for the New World," Gaja explains. "However, it's better for China not to copy the system mechanically but to create a new version based on its own history and nature and that takes time."

Gaja is probably the world's only well-known winery without its own website, he says.

"I don't like blowing my own horn but using word-of-mouth marketing. The best advertisement is placement of my wine on the wine lists of top restaurants," he says.

Gaja says that his own aesthetics and philosophy

— faithfully reflecting the land and respecting nature to the utmost — "is intrinsically contradictory to commercialized wine relying on manual intervention."

Angelo 酿出的 Nebbiolo 更像是个情商不高，恃才傲物的诗人，锋芒太露，性格过于强烈又不愿意修饰自己。

"人们总是嚷嚷着我种赤霞珠，其实它只占我种植面积的百分之二。我最爱的，永远是 Nebbiolo。" Angelo 说到这个葡萄品种，口气瞬间温柔下来。如果事先没有做过功课，真的会误以为他在说他的一个孩子。

紧接着，他话锋一转。以下的这段话让我相信，在这个世界上，没有人比他更懂得用浪漫而炙热的性生活来描述葡萄酒了：

"如果赤霞珠是一个男人，那么他每天都会在卧室里履行他该履行的职责，循规蹈矩，久而久之，也就没有新鲜感了；但 Nebbiolo 不同，很难解释为什么他深沉而安静地躲在角落里，透着份意味深长，永远参不透的复杂。"

用这样的葡萄酿出的酒，饱满、深沉、丰富，充满变化。

欧洲最负盛名的酒评家 Jancis Roinson 在她的品酒词里记录道：

Nebbiolo instead of Cabernet

"That means it's impossible for my wine to be perfect, since there's always some defect in nature. If a wine is described as perfect, I strongly suspect there's something gray behind it. It's just like a fashion models on magazine covers. If she looks perfect, the photo must have been retouched," he says.

"We need to appreciate the imperfections in wine and that's the elegance of fine wine," the vintner says.

Gaja caused a sensation in Italy by planting Cabernet Sauvignon in 1978, but it was his reinterpretation of Nebbiolo, once an obscure and cheap Italian variety, that established the global status of Barbaresco.

Gaja says that his experimentation with Cabernet has been exaggerated.

"它陈年后散发的香气，萦绕心头，深刻到难以忘记，让人仿佛置身秋天的灌木丛，身边围绕着玫瑰花、紫罗兰，又好像是在一堆点燃的木头旁边，感受到其飘散出的缕缕青烟。"

美国的酒评家 Robert Parker 的品酒词，虽然没那么浪漫，但更为直观："丹宁太强烈，年轻时让人难以接近。"

"我欣赏这份真实所带给人的震撼和触动。大自然总是有缺陷的，没有所谓完美的葡萄园，当然也就不存在完美的葡萄酒。我们应该学着去欣赏这份不完美，这恰恰是葡萄酒幽雅的真谛。" Angelo 说道。

在市场上，的确存在那些靠着人工修饰而获得的满分酒，但在他看来，这太做作，就像是被 photoshop 软件过度处理过的时尚杂志封面女郎。

人定胜天，本来就是一种浪漫的想象和不切实际的期待。但尊重自然不代表他不作为，更不意味着他对葡萄酒的质量有任何的妥协。

"Many people didn't notice that the Cabernet I planted only accounts for 2 percent of the vineyard. I like Nebbiolo much more."

"If Cabernet were a man, he would do his duty every night in the bedroom, but always the same way," Gaja says. "Nebbiolo, on the other hand, would be the brooding, quiet man in the corner, harder to understand but infinitely more complex."

Few grapes are like Nebbiolo, "full of extract and high sugar levels, balanced by great acidity," says Master of Wine Jancis Robinson, an influential wine critic.

"The wine is typically intensely aromatic, developing the most extraordinary haunting bouquet in which, variously, roses, autumn undergrowth, wood smoke, violets and tar can often be found ... the tannins are unyielding for the moment," Robinson writes.

The unyielding, hard-to-tame nature of the grape is a great challenge, both in the vineyard and the winery, Gaja says.

Angelo 坦陈，这十年来的全球气候变暖正重写着葡萄酒产业的游戏规则：

"整个夏天变得更加漫长，温暖而干燥，这倒是有利于葡萄成熟，酿出的酒品质也趋于稳定。但这也给葡萄园带来了新型的病虫害，我们老的那一套对付虫害的方法已经不管用了。"

He says the Nebbiolo vines are "as naturally vigorous as a runaway horse," adding that they must be sharply pruned so they don't waste energy sprouting leaves instead of ripening fruit.

Twenty-eight years after taking over his family business in 1961, Gaja pruned drastically, which made production tumble.

"People thought he was crazy and grape farmers snickered. For us the difference between Angelo and his father was just like day and night," says Luigi Cavallo-Gino, the most experienced grape farmer at Gaja Winery. He is quoted in Gaja's book "The Vines of San Lorenzo."

很多酒庄为此加大了化学肥料和杀虫剂的用量。Angelo 觉得这会对他最珍爱的土地造成不可弥补的伤害。

"我组建了一个全新的团队，成员包括了植物学家、地质学家和病虫害学家。他们正努力通过找到这些病虫的自然天敌来解决问题。"他说道。

这些问题虽然让他头疼，但也促使他不断地思考，保持着对葡萄园的激情。

Gaja's father worried that the heavy pruning and low yield would bankrupt the winery.

The son says the pruning and his new thinking was inspired by travels in France "where they respect wine from their heart," and the Napa Valley where they act with courage.